THE HEART OF *Prayer*

Reviews from the Pulpit

There are plenty of books on prayer, but *The Heart of Prayer: The Essential Guide to Knowing God through Prayer* by D.M. Stahlheber will definitely stand out. It is a great combination of the practical and theological and so appropriately named as it speaks to the heart of how and why we should pray. When the world and the church is confronting challenging times, this is a great book to get the church back on track and praying. This book is a blessing to the body of Christ, no matter where you are in your journey with Jesus.

—John Rivera
Pastor, Hope Tabernacle

There are many books on prayer on the market today; however, there seems to be a lack of teaching on how to pray—until now. *The Heart of Prayer* does just that. D. M. shares from her own experiences and testimony. She gives the reader insight and instruction on prayer and how we can interact with God on a deeper, more personal level. I recommend this book to anybody with a desire to learn the basics of prayer and to those who want to strengthen their prayer life.

—Ben Monk
Senior Pastor, Manchester Church of God

Prayer is at the heart of our relationship with God, and with her book, *The Heart of Prayer*. D. M. Stahlheber has captured the essence of how we can meaningfully connect and communicate with God. She deftly weaves together theological perspective with personal application as she considers how and why we pray. She helps us see that building a relationship with God is a process, and she gives us the biblical and practical tools needed to deepen our faith and draw closer to our Creator. This will be a valuable resource for those seeking to better understand the power of prayer.

Rebecca Mincieli

Reverend, John Wesley United Methodist Church

D. M. gets to the "heart" of the matter by showing how Scripture and the Holy Spirit connect God's heart to ours, unlocking the intimacy God intends for us in prayer. *The Heart of Prayer* encourages the reader into life-changing, purpose-realizing prayer, whether you've been a Christian all your life or just now exploring the faith.

—Bob McKenney

Senior Pastor, Bethany Chapel Community Church

This book is a gem! Whether you're just starting to build a prayer life or you're struggling to pray regularly or you're someone who has a solid and consistent prayer life, this book will inspire you to pray and pray more. More than just knowing the importance of prayer and understanding its power and value in our Christian walk, D. M. helps you see the heart of the Father, develop intimacy with the Holy Spirit, and fall in love with Jesus over and over again through prayer.

—Richie Cayabyab

Worship Pastor at Grace Capital Church

This book is exceptional. It was written with simplicity and yet it will encourage even those deepest in devotion to prayer. It is filled with a beautiful balance of Scripture, personal stories, and great quotations. The personal stories are beautifully transparent. I think this will bring much encouragement to others.

—Anita Perry
Former City Prayer Leader

THE HEART OF *Prayer*

THE ESSENTIAL GUIDE to Knowing God Through Prayer

D. M. STAHLHEBER

NASHVILLE

NEW YORK • LONDON • MELBOURNE • VANCOUVER

THE HEART OF *Prayer*

THE ESSENTIAL GUIDE to Knowing God Through Prayer

Published in New York, New York, by Morgan James Publishing. Morgan James is a trademark of Morgan James, LLC. www.MorganJamesPublishing.com

Proudly distributed by Ingram Publisher Services.

ISBN 978-1-63195-732-1 paperback
ISBN 978-1-63195-733-8 ebook
Library of Congress Control Number: 2021915286

Cover Design by:
Rachel Lopez
www.r2cdesign.com

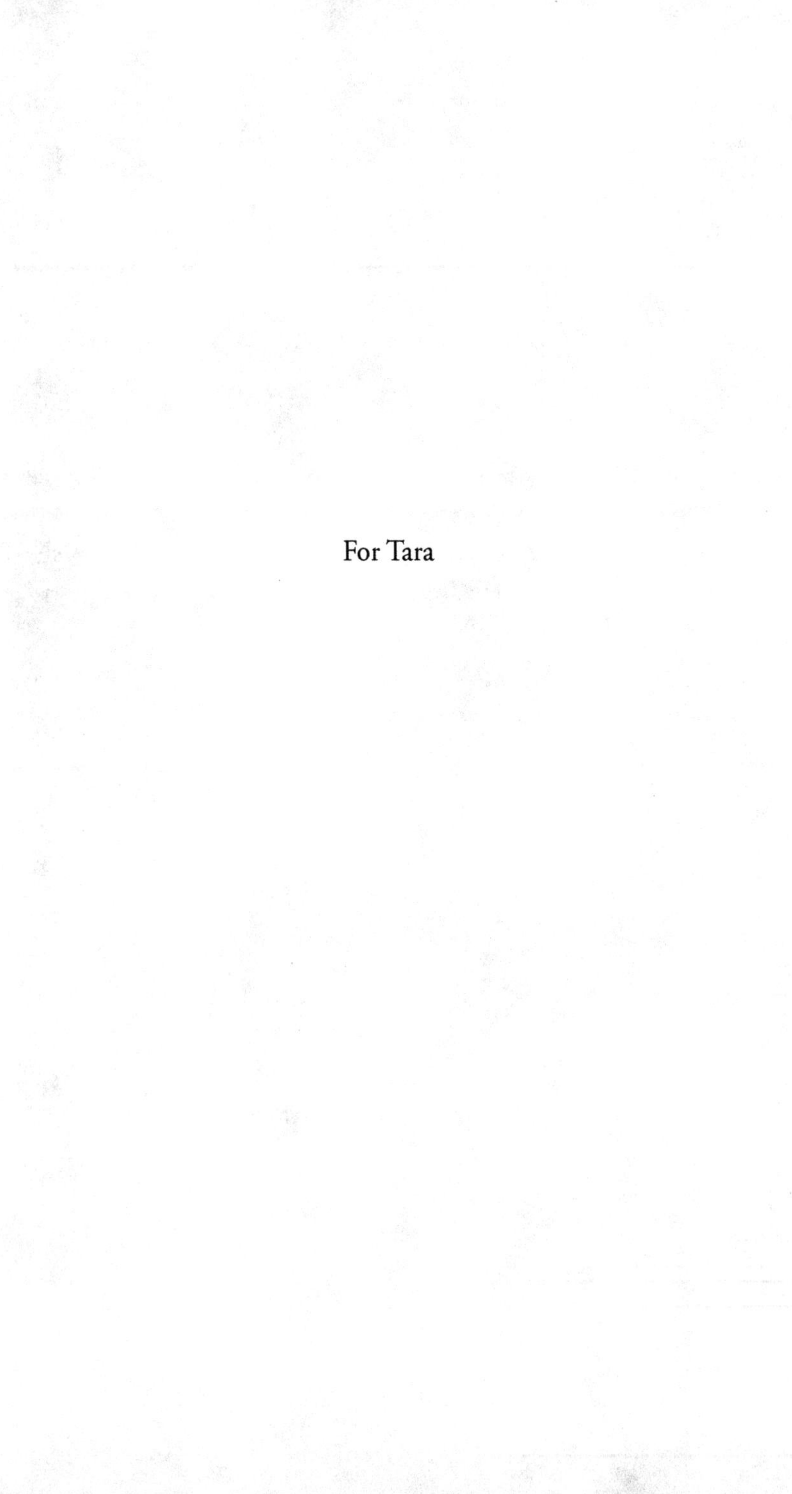

For Tara

Thanks be to God, who is my all in all, for directing and guiding this content and shaping my heart.

Thank you to my family for their love and support, which gives me courage.

Blessings to the pastors and ministry leaders who helped in directing this book.

Thank you also to Randy and Jill Thompson for providing a wonderful place of rest and access to excellent books with wonderful quotes.

CONTENTS

ACKNOWLEDGMENTS

For I, the Lord your God, hold your right hand; it is I who say to you, "Fear not, I am the one who helps you."
—Isaiah 41:13

The hand of God is powerful and has been my ever-present help, especially in writing this book. It is a constant effort to form a message and continue to refine it, especially on so holy a topic as prayer. I pray this text is pleasing to God. May he receive any and all glory for whatever comes from this endeavor.

This book, and any great effort I embark on, is made possible by my loving family whose continuous support gives me courage and hope to see it through to the end. In particular, my husband, daughter, and parents have been a steady encouragement, and I cannot thank them enough.

A good deal of gratitude is due to countless individuals of great faith who have led by example and generously shared with me many hours of teaching and conversation over the years. However, I extend a special thank you to the following pastors and leaders for their advice and affirmation of this book:

Reverend Rebecca Mincieli, Reverend Jason Wells, Pastor Ben Monk, Pastor John Rivera, Worship Leader Richie Cyabyab, and Pastor Bob McKenney.

It has been my enormous blessing to have the prayers of Evelyn Sullivan supporting me throughout this effort. She has been my lifeline over the years, and I am forever grateful to her for her love and support.

A special thank you to Anita Perry and Linda DeLorey for their additional supporting prayers over this book and other matters.

The book itself is made immensely better by the wisdom and experience of editor Jennifer Hanchey. Her skills have been a blessing in shaping the words of this book.

Thank you to Morgan James Publishing for believing in the power of prayer and for offering generous support and an exemplary publishing model that helps authors thrive.

May God bless you all.

Give thanks in all circumstances; for this is the will of God in Christ Jesus for you.

—1 Thessalonians 5:18

INTRODUCTION

Learning to pray, or seeking God's face, is a lifetime journey and not necessarily a one-and-done endeavor. This book is not meant to outline all there is to prayer nor should it be the sole resource for one hungry to know God.

The purpose of this book is to provide a solid groundwork for who God is and to encourage a heart-to-heart relationship with God through prayer. In and of itself, this book's teaching is simple: talk to God and listen for how he speaks back. No fluffy words, rigorous study, or years of practice are needed. Prayer comes from the heart.

One of the best ways to learn is through experience, so I highly recommend not only reading but also praying with others. This book focuses more on the individual's prayer practices, but whenever two or more are gathered, God is with us (Matt. 18:20). So prayer as a group is a great way to learn and be with God. If your church or community does not have a prayer group or house of prayer, you can join in prayer conference calls.

Prayer, being a conversation with God, can bring up some areas in need of healing and counsel. If you find yourself in such a position and feel overwhelmed, please reach out to your pastor or community church. I pray God will lead you to the right church and people to connect with.

This is a journey that we are not meant to do alone. God is love. Jesus loves us and prayed that we would love each other as he loves the Father (John 17:21–23). Through prayer and with our brothers and sisters in Christ, we can traverse this great pathway that leads to eternal life with our Creator.

I pray this book provides a foundation for a heart of prayer to grow in your life, that you might seek and find that God is good and ever present in your life. Amen.

STAGES OF PRAYER

Why is prayer important? Prayer is important because it is the way we communicate with God. How else can we get to know the God of all creation if we don't pray? It's like trying to make a friend but never talking to the person. Spending time together with God allows a relationship to grow and develop, as is true with a friend or colleague.

God's main goal is for us to know him. I once heard it said that if one were to sum up the Bible, it's essentially a story of how God wants his kids back. I always loved that explanation because the Bible truly does outline the story of God's massive love. He created human beings and all they would need, and then he watched them turn away from him as he constantly tried to guide them home to him again. A beautiful place in Barre, Massachusetts, called The Cross, was built by a devout Christian man who wrote in his fields using trees: "God's Wisdom says come back to me." God is calling us home to him. Will we draw near to him by responding in prayer?

The Bible is critical to our learning about God, and when we know him, we can love him. When we love him, we are complete and loved because God is love. We are his beloved, meaning it is our blessed purpose to be loved. All we need to do is ask him into our hearts and begin the journey of getting to know him through prayer and his Word.

This book is full of Scripture because the Bible is his Word and truth. It guides us through the good news of who God is. But the Word must be coupled with prayer. Otherwise, it's like reading a book about a celebrity but never actually talking to the celebrity. You won't really know what this person is truly like until you build a relationship, and with God, relationship is accomplished through prayer.

That the God of all creation wants to speak to us is a fact full of joy and wonder, yet we find, too often, our attempts to communicate with God seem ineffective. I wager this is because of our expectations and the state of our prayer life.

Everyone is at a different stage of prayer in building a relationship with God, and anyone can go through any of the stages. Prayer is a journey and a process of transformation. For those willing to undertake the journey, the way is filled with wonder and awe but also, at times, frustration and discomfort. Know that it's worth it.

Let's outline the stages of prayer to illustrate a few ways we might see prayer manifest in the church. Please don't take this to mean anything is wrong with being in these particular stages. In fact, it's quite common to be in stage 1 or 2 for awhile in your quest to know God. My goal is that people will be encouraged by understanding what a prayer life could be and will, therefore, seek to grow ever deeper in their prayer life.

Stage 1: Mail to Santa

Many people start out seeing prayer like writing a letter to Santa. A request is written a few times a year and dropped into the mailbox (atmosphere). It is sent somewhere vague, somewhere near the North Pole (heaven), and the sender doesn't fully trust it will get there. Then the sender hopes that if they are good enough, one day this request will be answered with the gift they asked for (answered prayer).

This stage is the beginning of a prayer walk and can be frustrating to many beginners because it is a misunderstanding of the love God would bestow upon them. He so desperately desires to hear from us and speak to us, but this kind of prayer leaves no room for closeness. A relationship is slow to grow through mail and much can be missed over time.

Also, sometimes the answers to a "Santa" prayer cannot be found because we hold an expectation of how it will be wrapped, that it will be answered exactly how it was requested. Our God is so big and wonderful that he knows all things and what is best. Sometimes he answers our prayers in different ways, but those believers in the mail to Santa stage leave no room for alternative answers. Therefore, the answers are often completely missed. The person praying can become discouraged and think God is not answering their prayers when, in actuality, he has heard and responded in a different way.

It is okay to be at this stage, but moving into a closer relationship will bring increased joy. It is wise to move on from here as quickly as possible. Chapter 10 outlines ways to grow in prayer, like making time to pray and develop greater levels of devotion to God.

Stage 2: Phone Call

Others approach prayer like a phone call. Those in this stage will pick up the phone and leave a voice message with demands, asking for needs to be met.

Or they might pick up the phone and hang it back up while he's talking because they are busy or distracted.

Or some pick up the phone, hear a few things, and then go research what it might mean, not returning for days to ask him what he meant.

We all want to connect with God, but our approach is often one-sided or filled with distractions that keep us from having a deeper relationship with God or hearing what he would say to us.

The phone call approach also leaves no room for God's reply. I've heard it said that God responds to prayer; the answers are often yes, no, yes but not how you expect, or yes but not yet. These answers are missed when we are distracted or worried; we don't hear or notice what he is trying to share.

Again, this is a normal phase for many Christians, but I would challenge you to go deeper with the Lord by opening your heart with humility, seeking repentance and forgiveness. We'll talk about how to do this in chapter 12.

Stage 3: Sitting at His Feet

A few approach prayer like sitting at Jesus' feet, listening and waiting like Mary in Luke 10. While Mary sits at the

Lord's feet, putting his words first, Martha is busy with the distractions of life. Though worries and chores are valid concerns, they are not more important than our God. Jesus says Mary has chosen better, not because he is arrogant or an attention seeker but because he knows that what he is teaching and saying will help her through life and draw her closer to him. And ultimately, he longs to be reunited in friendship and love with his people.

Let's consider Luke 10:38–42 together:

> As Jesus and his disciples were on their way, he came to a village where a woman named Martha opened her home to him. She had a sister called Mary, who sat at the Lord's feet listening to what he said. But Martha was distracted by all the preparations that had to be made. She came to him and asked, "Lord, don't you care that my sister has left me to do the work by myself? Tell her to help me!" "Martha, Martha," the Lord answered, "you are worried and upset about many things, but few things are needed—or indeed only one. Mary has chosen what is better, and it will not be taken away from her" (NIV).

In many cases, those who sit at his feet have done a lot of the hard work and "heart work" that it takes to remove distraction, barriers, and long-rooted issues, which allows them to freely trust and seek the Lord, listening to his every word and instruction. This is the result of a long and loving relationship in prayer with God.

Listening, discerning, and trusting God will help us get to the place of sitting at his feet in prayer. We'll discuss these concepts in-depth in chapter 13.

Stage 4: Walking in the Garden

Then there are the rare few who will walk with God as friends, hearing a live conversation and talking in the shade of the evening as Adam and Eve did in the garden: "Then the man and his wife heard the sound of the LORD God as he was walking in the garden in the cool of the day, and they hid from the LORD God among the trees of the garden. But the LORD God called to the man, 'Where are you?' He answered, 'I heard you in the garden, and I was afraid because I was naked; so I hid'" (Gen. 3:8–10, NIV).

These verses from Genesis highlight that Adam and Eve could clearly hear God as he walked in the same garden that they cared for. This is the kind of closeness—hearing and walking in step with God—that a robust prayer life and deep heart work can bring, but few seek it or are willing to do the heart work necessary to get to this stage. This is the desired stage of prayer the God of all creation originally designed us to have, and it is his great joy to give it to us now.

Which type of prayer life would you like? It's okay to be in the beginning stages. We all pass through those early understandings of prayer as our walk with God is a journey. But be encouraged that there is a path forward if we are willing to open our hearts to God and let him in. The pages to come will illuminate a path to bring you from one stage to another. Prayer is a wonderful gift from God, but it is also something that comes from the heart. It requires effort and devotion as you will read in subsequent chapters, but the reward is worth it.

Part 1

A FOUNDATION FOR PRAYER

Chapter 1

HEART-TO-HEART WITH GOD: WHAT IS PRAYER?

To pray is to walk in the full light of God and to say simply, without holding back, "I am human and you are God."[1]
—Henri Nouwen, *With Open Hands*

To me, prayer is a heart-to-heart conversation with God. The God of all creation wants to speak to us, and he uses prayer as his means of communication to connect us to his love. I like how Albert Day puts it in his book, *The Captivating Presence.* He writes of God's constant desire to connect with us, though he is fully aware of our sin:

> He is forever trying to establish communication; forever aware of the wrong directions we are taking and wishing to warn us; forever offering solutions for the problems that baffle us; forever standing at the door of our loneliness, eager to bring us such comradeship as the most intelligent living mortal could not supply;

> forever clinging to our indifference in the hope that someday our needs, or at least our tragedies will waken us to respond to his advances.[2]

Essentially, God is trying to communicate with us. He is aware of our fumbling and wrongdoing and wants to help us with all our struggles. He is eager to draw us into an intimate relationship because he knows that he alone can know us deeply and provide what we need. But it requires our communication with him, which is done primarily through prayer.

The communication vehicle we use is prayer because it helps us to learn about God, just as we learn from our friends through conversation. As we learn about God through prayer and reading Scripture, with help from the Holy Spirit, we can know him, and to know God is to love him: "Anyone who does not love does not know God, because God is love." (1 John 4:8).

Many people I've spoken with are intimidated by prayer. They fear they'll need to know all the right words or memorize Scripture by heart; thus, they become discouraged before they even start. Some think prayer requires skill, but I'm happy to say that it does not. If you can talk to a family member or loved one, you can talk to God. He understands everyday language and does not require flowery words or poetry. He is happy to hear from you in any way. He is the Creator of language and knows our heart better than we do, so he knows what we mean by our words.

Prayer can be as simple as a few honest words with your Creator. And it's okay to share in your own unique style, even using your sense of humor. Since we are created in God's image, we know that he has a sense of humor too. He's walked with believers since the dawn of time and has heard and seen it all. So don't be afraid to speak your mind or share your true thoughts. Prayer is a heart-to-heart conversation with your Creator who loves you.

The Lord's Prayer

Jesus' own disciples wanted to know how to pray. So he gave them an excellent guide for prayer. We can find this guide in Matthew 6:9–13, now called the Lord's Prayer. He said we should ask that God would forgive our sins, bring his Kingdom, provide for our needs, and helps us when temptation is set before us. God can do all these things, knowing we are weak and limited in our view of the full picture he designed and knows: "This, then, is how you should pray: 'Our Father in heaven, hallowed be your name, your Kingdom come, your will be done, on earth as it is in heaven. Give us today our daily bread. And forgive us our debts, as we also have forgiven our debtors. And lead us not into temptation, but deliver us from the evil one'" (NIV).

The Lord's Prayer contains key elements some people use as their model for prayer. Seeking God's will and not our own, asking that his Kingdom would come to earth as it is in heaven, and forgiving as he forgave are all key elements here. We will talk about forgiveness later on in chapter 12 of this book. It is good to have a model as we think about strengthening our prayer life. Each time we approach God, we would do well to ask for his will to be done to change our world and our hearts that we would not be taken in by evil but live as in God's Kingdom while here on earth.

Matthew 6:9–13 is also a great outline or "go-to" prayer in a time of need. It's quite amazing that as we pray, listening and obeying God, the answer to his prayer comes, for we do the work of the Kingdom and his will through our obedience: "Your Kingdom come, your will be done."

This is a beautiful way to capture the essence and results of prayer, for we get to commune with the most creative and loving being of all, one so generous as to share his visions, thoughts, and ideas with mortal man. And this is through a loving relationship using prayer.

As we love him, our hearts are made new, and we draw closer to him, accessing the fullness of freedom and salvation that he died on the cross for us to receive.

Chapter 2

MADE TO PRAY: WHY DO WE PRAY?

To be a Christian without prayer is no more possible than to be alive without breathing.[3]

—Martin Luther

As noted, we pray to know God, and to know God is to love God. At the very heart of prayer is a true, authentic relationship with the God of all things. However, our God is so loving and abundant, he gives even more blessings through a powerful prayer life. Scripture outlines the many benefits to prayer, so we'll spend time together studying the verses that refer to prayer.

In *The Spiritual Life,* John H. Westerhoff III and John D. Eusden write that through prayer, we learn our identity in God and receive direction for our lives, and we are being continually transformed by this process. They even go so far to say that "prayer is a disciplined dedication to paying attention." The text implies that part of our natural design is to pray or commune with our God.[4]

> Our primary orientation can be an institution or some great cause or even other people, but first and forever, we must seek to know God. Unless our identity is hidden in God, we will never know who we are or what we are to do. Our first act must be prayer… Prayer is a disciplined dedication to paying attention. Without the single-minded attentiveness of prayer, we will rarely hear anything worth repeating or catch a vision worth asking anyone else to gaze upon.[5]

Prayer requires certain action, dedication, and attention as the above quote outlines, and we will discuss these elements in part II of this book. Prayer is, at the core, a beautiful way our hearts commune with the heart of God.

The many reasons to pray are given throughout the Bible. One reason we pray is because we are in need. We live in a world of darkness and difficulty, but God loves us and wants to help us navigate this challenging world if we seek him. We pray because we want to know him more; we pray for healing; we pray for any number of things. But at the heart of all prayer is a desire, a hunger to know God and be loved by him.

He is ever looking for us to ask for his help so that he may respond as Savior. He is a God who has given everything to us, even his only Son (John 3:16). He holds nothing back (Rom. 8:32). Prayer is a conduit for his blessings and gifts. In the Bible, we see that he helps in the time of need:

- "Is anyone among you in trouble? Let them pray. Is anyone happy? Let them sing songs of praise" (Jas. 5:13, NIV).
- "Answer me when I call to you, my righteous God. Give me relief from my distress; have mercy on me and hear my prayer" (Ps. 4:1, NIV).

It is when we seek him and look to him that he is able to help us. Because God listens to us, he cares about what is happening in our hearts and in our land. This is made evident in 2 Chronicles 7:12–16:

> Then the LORD appeared to Solomon in the night and said to him: "I have heard your prayer and have chosen this place for myself as a house of sacrifice. When I shut up the heavens so that there is no rain, or command the locust to devour the land, or send pestilence among my people, if my people who are called by my name humble themselves, and pray and seek my face and turn from their wicked ways, then I will hear from heaven and will forgive their sin and heal their land. Now my eyes will be open and my ears attentive to the prayer that is made in this place. For now I have chosen and consecrated this house that my name may be there forever. My eyes and my heart will be there for all time."

If we come in a humble manner, seeking his face, praying and turning from our wicked ways with a heart of repentance, then he will forgive our sin and heal our land. This is so powerful. In God's great grace and mercy, he offers this to us, but we must pray and do some heart work so that we are in a place to turn from our wicked ways and come with a repentant heart.

God knows the enemy (Satan) seeks to deceive us, but God wants to give us life and to save us through his steadfast love. He does not give meagerly but in abundance, as it says in John 10:10: "The thief comes only to steal and kill and destroy. I came that they may have life and have it abundantly."

There are so many reasons to pray and all for our benefit. Read on for more Scripture verses that outline powerful reasons to pray.

Scriptures to Aid in Prayer

The following verses outline the value and benefits of prayer. As each of these verses contains so much meaning, I encourage you to read the entire chapter from which it is pulled. Study the chapter to better understand its context, and then seek the Lord in prayer to gain insight. You may notice I repeat some of these verses throughout this book because they are so relevant and powerful.

- **We pray to put our requests before God:** "Do not be anxious about anything, but in everything by prayer and supplication with thanksgiving let your requests be made known to God" (Phil. 4:6).
- **We pray, for as we abide and God's Word lives in us, we may receive our requests:** "If you abide in me, and

my words abide in you, ask whatever you wish, and it will be done for you" (John 15:7).

- **We pray because it is God's will that we rejoice, pray, and give thanks in all circumstances:** "Rejoice always, pray without ceasing, give thanks in all circumstances; for this is the will of God in Christ Jesus for you" (1 Thess. 5:16–18).
- **We pray because the Spirit will intercede for us:** "Likewise the Spirit helps us in our weakness. For we do not know what to pray for as we ought, but the Spirit himself intercedes for us with groanings too deep for words" (Rom. 8:26).
- **We pray for healing:** "Therefore, confess your sins to one another and pray for one another, that you may be healed. The prayer of a righteous person has great power as it is working" (Jas. 5:16).
- **We pray to receive, to find, and for doors to be opened:** "And I tell you, ask, and it will be given to you; seek, and you will find; knock, and it will be opened to you" (Luke 11:9).
- **We pray because God may share great and hidden things:** "Call to me and I will answer you, and will tell you great and hidden things that you have not known" (Jer. 33:3).
- **We pray to avoid temptation:** "Watch and pray that you may not enter into temptation. The spirit indeed is willing, but the flesh is weak" (Matt. 26:41).

- **We pray that God would hear and deliver us:** "When the righteous cry for help, the Lord hears and delivers them out of all their troubles" (Ps. 34:17).
- **We pray that God might forgive our sins and heal our land:** "If my people who are called by my name humble themselves, and pray and seek my face and turn from their wicked ways, then I will hear from heaven and will forgive their sin and heal their land" (2 Chron. 7:14).
- **We pray because God is among us when two or more are gathered:** "Again I say to you, if two of you agree on earth about anything they ask, it will be done for them by my Father in heaven. For where two or three are gathered in my name, there am I among them" (Matt. 18:19–20).

Prayer can do all of these things and more, but most important, God loves us and wants to know us through prayer. He wants to know what is on our hearts, what gives us joy, and what makes us sad—everything. He is always there to provide wisdom and strength, courage and peace; it's all because of his great love for us. Prayer is the key. He wants us to commune with him, and out of his great love, he will help us, rejoice with us, and provide for us in our times of trouble. Hold fast to the promise of Jeremiah 29:12: "Then you will call on me and come and pray to me, and I will listen to you."

And Psalm 145:18 reminds us that "The LORD is near to all who call on him, to all who call on him in truth." We see that prayer draws God near to us. Isn't that wonderful? He wants to be near us, and we get to enjoy his presence through the gift of prayer. But why would we want to draw near to God? Who is he that we would want to know him? Some may not have heard of this God or might have some preconceived ideas of who he is. In the following chapters, we will outline who God is as noted in the Scriptures.

Chapter 3
GOD THE HOLY TRINITY: WHO IS GOD?

The Divine Heart is an ocean full of all good things, wherein poor souls can cast all their needs; it is an ocean full of joy to drown all our sadness, an ocean of humility to drown our folly, and an ocean of mercy to those in distress, an ocean of love in which to submerge our poverty. [6]

—St. Margaret Mary Alacoque

Our God is a Holy Trinity made up of three persons: God the Father, God the Son (Jesus Christ), and God the Holy Spirit. Think of it like a family. Each of these three members is unique, and together they are powerful, constantly working in unison for our good (Rom. 8:28). As with humans, a son resembles the father in design and thinking, yet the son is separate. As God is perfect in every way, the Son is the truest nature of the Father (John 14:9, NIV). The Holy Spirit is the third person of the Trinity, and he is God's Holy Spirit that connects us to the heart of God. The Spirit is our Helper as

John 14:26 tells us: "But the Advocate, the Holy Spirit, whom the Father will send in my name, will teach you all things and will remind you of everything I have said to you" (NIV).

Yet, in all these forms, God is one; there is no other. The Nicene Creed is a beautiful expression of the triune God we serve. God is three but one; no other is above him:

The Nicene Creed
We believe in one God,
the Father almighty,
maker of heaven and earth,
of all things visible and invisible.
And in one Lord Jesus Christ,
the only Son of God,
begotten from the Father before all ages,
God from God,
Light from Light,
true God from true God,
begotten, not made;
of the same essence as the Father.
Through him all things were made.
For us and for our salvation
he came down from heaven;
he became incarnate by the Holy Spirit and the virgin Mary,
and was made human.
He was crucified for us under Pontius Pilate;
he suffered and was buried.
The third day he rose again, according to the Scriptures.
He ascended to heaven

and is seated at the right hand of the Father.
He will come again with glory
to judge the living and the dead.
His Kingdom will never end.
And we believe in the Holy Spirit,
the Lord, the giver of life.
He proceeds from the Father and the Son,
and with the Father and the Son is worshiped and glorified.
He spoke through the prophets.
We believe in one holy catholic and apostolic church.
We affirm one baptism for the forgiveness of sins.
We look forward to the resurrection of the dead,
and to life in the world to come. Amen.

God Is Love

God is love. Through prayer we are empowered to love others with that same love. In *With Open Hands*, Henri Nouwen writes, "At the moment that you fully realize that the God who loves you unconditionally loves all your fellow human beings with the same love, a new way of living opens itself to you. For you come to see with new eyes those who live beside you in this world."[7]

The overall theme in this powerful Trinity is love. Understanding God's nature as love is a necessary part of understanding why prayer is so closely linked to the heart. Theologian Frederick Buechner wrote of this:

> Love is not a faucet to be turned on or off at will. God himself doesn't just love me or you, he is love...That

> is his identity, and explains why he loves individuals, even when he is not pleased with them. We are directed by Paul to "be imitators of God, as beloved children; and walk in love, just as Christ also loved you and gave himself up for us" (Eph. 5:1–2). We are called and enabled to love as God loves.[8]

And if our primary purpose is to be loved and to love others (Mark 12:30–31), then it is significant that God is a person who is love and can be loved, as Miroslov Volf wrote in his book, *A Public Faith*,

> First, he [Augustine] believed that God is not an impersonal Reason dispersed throughout the world but a "person" who loves and can be loved in return. Second, to be human is to love; we can choose what to love but not whether to love. Third, we live well when we love both God and neighbor, aligning ourselves with the God who loves. Fourth, we will flourish and be truly happy when we discover joy in loving the infinite God and our neighbors in God.[9]

In order to pray, we need to answer the question, who is God? Why is this question essential? Because it is too easy to make God into someone domesticated, powerless, angry, or false, someone based on our preconceived notions. C. S. Lewis illustrates this beautifully in his series, *The Chronicles of Narnia*.[10] Aslan, the lion and Christ-figure, is not a "tame" lion. He is still very much a wild animal, however good and kind. Likewise, our God is not tame; he is not controlled or limited by our ideas. He is powerful, mighty, and strong yet tenderhearted and full of righteousness and mercy. He is to be feared as the one true God and treated with a deep reverence, yet he also calls himself son of man, dying so that the Godhead could be approachable without the law that Moses brought to the Israelites.

We have access to him now because of Jesus' sacrifice, but we use prayer to fully realize this access. "The basis of true prayer as well as its goal" is knowing who God is, according to Donald G. Bloesch in his book, *The Struggle of Prayer*:

> Christian prayer rests upon the irreversible fact of the self-revelation of God in Jesus Christ and its confirmation in our hearts by the Holy Spirit. The Holy Trinity is the basis of true prayer as well as its goal. Prayer, as biblical faith understands it, is made possible by the triune God and is directed to this God. To gain a true awareness of the depth and breadth of Christian prayer, it is necessary to understand something of the nature of the God who originates such prayer. This God is first of all a Personal Spirit who is self-sustaining and who is the ground of everything that is. He not only exists but he also coexists as a Trinity. He is capable of having fellowship with humanity because he has fellowship within himself. He is capable of caring because he embodies love within himself.[11]

Understanding that God is love is crucial to understanding the nature of God and his Word. Scripture is only as good as the heart with which we come to it. If we are already thinking God is angry, we will see him in Scripture as angry. This is our own perspective skewing the truth of who the Bible says God is. God *is* love. Love is not something he can be separated from. Love is patient, and love is kind. In 1 Corinthians 13, we see the shape of God's love.

We also see that God disciplines those he loves, which makes discipline another form of love. It's not always fun to be disciplined, but we know it helps us grow. A loving parent will not let their child do things that will lead to pain or suffering if they can help it. Do not touch fire, do not run in front of a moving vehicle, we tell our children. We discipline rebellious children because we know it will help them grow into thoughtful and loving adults. God is love, so everything he does has love at its core and is informed by his infinite wisdom and grace.

The Word of God gives us amazing and various descriptions of the Father, the Son, and the Holy Spirit. Not everything will be touched upon in the following pages, but my summary of each facet of our triune God will give you a basic understanding of the Trinity. Going forward, as you pray, you will find the sense of the Holy Trinity's presence grows as each member becomes more and more real to you. I pray each will reveal himself to you as you explore, for the Trinity is limitless. There is no end to the depths of what we can discover about God.

Chapter 4

GOD THE FATHER

Whoever does not love does not know God, because God is love. This is how God showed his love among us: He sent his one and only Son into the world that we might live through him. This is love: not that we loved God, but that he loved us and sent his Son as an atoning sacrifice for our sins.

—1 John 4:8–10, NIV

This is the message we have heard from him and declare to you: God is light; in him there is no darkness at all.

—1 John 1:5, NIV

God the Father loves us so much that he gave his only son to die for our sins (John 3:16). He is the "source," the originator of all: "Yet for us there is one God, the Father, from whom are all things and for whom we exist, and one Lord, Jesus Christ, through whom are all things and through whom we exist" (1 Cor. 8:6).

Many movies and stories these days depict the Creator of the universe as cruel, unjust, selfish, and maniacal, though this could not be further from the truth. Even children's movies depict a selfish and cruel father. In *Harry Potter and the Sorcerer's Stone,* Uncle Vernon is a father who spoils his own son but treats Harry, his nephew, spitefully.[12] Some TV shows depict fathers as uncaring, absent, or abusive. Of course, these things do happen in many families, but if these are the only depictions of fathers we see portrayed in media, then how could we possibly imagine a Father God who is loving? If we did not have a good relationship with our own father while growing up, it's easy to develop a skewed perception of our Creator.

The 2014 stats from the US Census Bureau says 23.6 percent of children live in father-absent homes.[13] This means that almost a quarter of the population is being raised without a male role model in their daily lives. This doesn't even account for parents who might be physically present but emotionally absent because of substance abuse or financial or marital stress.

Fortunately, God the Father is a good father. He is not only our origin but is also deeply in love with us today. He is so in love with us that he gave us his only Son. John 3:16 is a beloved verse, but we often forget the next verse where it says that Jesus came not to condemn the world but to save it (my paraphrase). Our God loved us so much that Jesus was sent to save us from our sin so that we could draw near to him: "For God so loved the world, that he gave his only Son, that whoever believes in him should not perish but have eternal life. For God did not send his Son into the world to condemn the world, but in order that the world might be saved through him" (John 3:16–17).

This love can be challenging to understand, not only because of our own personal experiences but also because of how we read or understand the Old Testament. When we forget God's great love, the Old Testament could be read as if God is angry or full of wrath toward his people.

As mentioned earlier, it's important to read the Bible with an understanding that God *is* love. It's not just something he does; he *is* love. Love cannot be separated from his nature, for God is the very embodiment of love. It's all out of love. What is astounding is that he made us his children. The Father would not be called a father if he did not have offspring. We are his children, and he loves us:

> For all who are led by the Spirit of God are sons of God. For you did not receive the spirit of slavery to fall back into fear, but you have received the Spirit of adoption as sons, by whom we cry, "Abba! Father!" The Spirit himself bears witness with our spirit that we are children of God, and if children, then heirs—heirs of God and fellow heirs with Christ, provided we suffer with him in order that we may also be glorified with him (Rom. 8:14–17).

Sometimes it is hard to understand the Father's love because part of loving your children is to discipline them. If we view the Scriptures, especially those in the Old Testament, from a view of a good parent disciplining his child, we can see love in his dealing with wayward Israel. As Proverbs 3:11–12 says, "My child, don't reject the Lord's discipline, and don't be upset when he corrects you. For the Lord corrects those he loves, just as a father corrects a child in whom he delights" (NLT). Our Father in heaven corrects us in love so that we learn his love.

God our Father made us and ordained all our days before birth. He has always existed, and he knew who we were before we were born:

> For you created my inmost being; you knit me together in my mother's womb. I praise you because I am fearfully and wonderfully made; your works are wonderful, I know that full well. My frame was not hidden from you when I was made in the secret place, when I was woven together in the depths of the earth. Your eyes saw my unformed body; all the days ordained for me were written in your book before one of them came to be (Ps. 139: 13–16, NIV).

A strong father is a teacher. He keeps his children in line and is a guide. Like the Lord God in the wilderness, he will carry his child when he or she cannot walk: "And in the wilderness where you saw how the LORD your God carried you, just as a man carries his son, in all the way which you have walked until you came to this place" (Deut. 1:31).

However, if one thinks about being a parent of children who do not have any rules or laws, what might discipline look like? Israel was lawless for a time and then, even with the law that God gave Moses, they rebelled. God disciplines those he loves so that they will grow rightly and be responsible, mature adults. God disciplined the Israelites and those in the Old Testament, always providing and showing great grace and mercy when his children disobeyed and did terrible things.

We have a loving Father in God, who looks after us, watches over us, disciplines us, and teaches us. All we need to do is draw near, seek and find, ask, and knock. We will then receive, and the door will be opened (Matt. 7:7). He has held nothing back from us, giving his only Son to be sacrificed that we could know him. For it is through Jesus' life on earth that we are able to see more of our Father's character and nature.

Testimony on God the Father

I was blessed with wonderful adoptive parents. My father is an amazing man but was incredibly busy as he provided for our family. He traveled a lot and had to work late hours to care for us and help a number of people at the vast businesses he worked for. We were very proud of him, but I didn't realize until later that how I experienced my father colored my image of God the Father.

I thought of God the Father as I thought of my dad: on his throne somewhere in heaven, busy with the entire world and universe. So I presumed that I should be careful not to bother God as I did not bother my preoccupied father. This couldn't be further from the truth. God the Father is orchestrating all things for us to know him, the Son, and the Holy Spirit. He wants us near and is ever present in our lives, looking over every detail.

I pray God will remove any false notions of God the Father from your life, if he hasn't already, and replace them with the truth of his enduring and steadfast love for you. Amen.

Chapter 5
GOD THE SON, JESUS CHRIST

In the beginning was the Word, and the Word was with God, and the Word was God.

—John 1:1

And the Word became flesh and dwelt among us, and we have seen his glory, glory as of the only Son from the Father, full of grace and truth.

—John 1:14

Jesus is the Son of God and also referred to in the Bible as the Word, who was with God in the beginning. He was with God before he was born in the flesh through the Holy Spirit and Mary. The Bible says he is King, a Holy Priest, our Kinsman Redeemer, our brother, and Friend. He was born to be the Savior of the world, freeing us from the law, fulfilling the prophesies in the Old Testament, even the prophesies about his suffering. He died on the cross and rose again on the third day, later ascending into heaven. This proved that he had the power to save us from death: "And we have seen and testify that the Father has sent his Son to be the Savior of the world. If anyone acknowledges that Jesus is the Son of God, God lives in them and they in God" (1 John 4:14–15).

Someone I met said that they struggled to relate to God the Father, but Jesus was easy to love for his sacrifice and display of love on the cross, which was so beautiful and full of grace. He laid down his very life to save us, having done nothing wrong himself.

Jesus' life clearly fulfilled the Old Testament Scriptures, revealing himself to be the Messiah, a title so highly contested with the religious scholars of his day that they had him crucified. The power of his life is in the way he lived and his resurrection after death. Reading the Bible gives us a clear picture of his goodness, faithfulness, and love for us. Without him, we have no salvation and no way to the Father (Acts 4:11–12). In order to understand the Father, we need to know Jesus and accept him; otherwise, we cannot possibly make our way to the Father. Remember John 14:6: "Jesus said to him, 'I am the way, and the truth, and the life. No one comes to the Father except through me.'"

His greatest desire is that we know him, for he shows us the way to the Father, leading us in truth and giving us life everlasting. Jesus is the great mediator; always interceding on our behalf: "For there is one God, and there is one mediator between God and men, the man Christ Jesus" (1 Tim. 2:5).

He is ever there to help us, watching over us and guiding us. Even David knew this and would look to God for his help: "I lift up my eyes to the mountains—where does my help come from? My help comes from the LORD, the Maker of heaven and earth. He will not let your foot slip—he who watches over you will not slumber" (Ps. 121:1–3, NIV).

Jesus is also love and light as he is the Son from the Father who is love and light: "Again Jesus spoke to them, saying, "I am the light of the world. Whoever follows me will not walk in darkness, but will have the light of life" (John 8:12). In this dark world we live in Jesus shines brightly, giving us hope and clearly directing our paths.

Jesus is the Son of God, the one who came to save us and who is our Lord and King. He is all-powerful and the Bridegroom to the church. He is the head of the church and a mighty leader for all his people, the Lord of heavenly hosts. He came to give us life, for we were condemned to death because of the sin in our lives. But Jesus died for our sins and now we are free: "The thief comes only to steal and kill and destroy. I came that they may have life and have it abundantly" (John 10:10).

Through Jesus' ascension to be with the Father, we are able to receive the Holy Spirit who lives and resides with and in us: "But the Helper, the Holy Spirit, whom the Father will send in my name, he will teach you all things and bring to your remembrance all that I have said to you" (John 14:26).

And as we are baptized with hearts of repentance in the name of Jesus Christ, we can receive the gift of the Holy Spirit: "And Peter said to them, 'Repent and be baptized every one of you in the name of Jesus Christ for the forgiveness of your sins, and you will receive the gift of the Holy Spirit'" (Acts 2:38).

If you haven't asked Jesus into your heart, this is a great opportunity to do so. Some like to use a formal prayer, but essentially, it's about believing with your heart that he was raised from the dead and confessing with your mouth that Jesus is Lord as you read in Romans 10:8–10:

But what does it say? "The word is near you, in your mouth and in your heart" (that is, the word of faith that we proclaim); because, if you confess with your mouth that Jesus is Lord and believe in your heart that God raised him from the dead, you will be saved. For with the heart one believes and is justified, and with the mouth one confesses and is saved.

Or others like to use Psalm 51:1–19 from King David as a template of asking for salvation:

> Have mercy on me, O God, according to your steadfast love; according to your abundant mercy blot out my transgressions. Wash me thoroughly from my iniquity, and cleanse me from my sin! For I know my transgressions, and my sin is ever before me. Against you, you only, have I sinned and done what is evil in your sight, so that you may be justified in your words and blameless in your judgment. Behold, I was brought forth in iniquity, and in sin did my mother conceive me. Behold, you delight in truth in the inward being, and you teach me wisdom in the secret heart. Purge me with hyssop, and I shall be clean; wash me, and I shall be whiter than snow. Let me hear joy and gladness; let the bones that you have broken rejoice. Hide your face from my sins, and blot out all my iniquities. Create in me a clean heart, O God, and renew a right spirit within me. Cast me not away from

> your presence, and take not your Holy Spirit from me. Restore to me the joy of your salvation, and uphold me with a willing spirit. Then I will teach transgressors your ways, and sinners will return to you. Deliver me from bloodguiltiness, O God, O God of my salvation, and my tongue will sing aloud of your righteousness. O Lord, open my lips, and my mouth will declare your praise. For you will not delight in sacrifice, or I would give it; you will not be pleased with a burnt offering. The sacrifices of God are a broken spirit; a broken and contrite heart, O God, you will not despise. Do good to Zion in your good pleasure; build up the walls of Jerusalem; then will you delight in right sacrifices, in burnt offerings and whole burnt offerings; then bulls will be offered on your altar.

God knows your heart and will receive whatever words you say in truth. He will come into your heart and bring the Holy Spirit.

Testimony on Jesus

Jesus seems the easiest to relate to in some ways, for he was born as a man, and we have his words recorded in Scripture. Yet, I found his words puzzling and difficult to understand at times because I often came with my experience as my own truth against his. He too can seem mercurial in some Scriptures, speaking in parables and rebuking the religious scholars of his day. It's often like a text message. When you read the words without the heart of the person coming through their tone of voice, you perceive the meaning in your own way, which may not be what was originally intended.

I think I often read Scripture regarding Jesus through my own filter. His words could seem harsh or challenging instead of loving and caring because that's how I treated myself. My own low self-esteem colored the way I thought Jesus' words were being spoken. Now I have asked the Holy Spirit to dwell in my life in a bigger way, and the Spirit guides me through the Bible.

Reading about Jesus is all about understanding his heart of love for us, a heart that was willing to die sacrificially in one of the most excruciating and painful ways known to man.

I pray that your reading of the Bible will be in truth and love, that you will be able to see the true heart of the words and allow them to draw you closer to the God who loves you. Amen.

Chapter 6
GOD THE HOLY SPIRIT

We need loving communication, we need the presence of the Spirit. That is why I do not believe in theologians who do not pray, who are not in humble communication of love with God. Neither do I believe in the existence of any human power to pass on authentic knowledge of God. Only God can speak about himself, and only the Holy Spirit, who is love, can communicate this knowledge to us.[14]

—Carlo Carretto, *The God Who Comes*

As the sacred Spirit of God who lives within us once we receive Christ, the Holy Spirit is critical to our relationship with God the Father and Jesus. The following verses allude to the importance of the Spirit in believers' lives:

- "And Peter said to them, 'Repent and be baptized every one of you in the name of Jesus Christ for the

forgiveness of your sins, and you will receive the gift of the Holy Spirit'" (Acts 2:38).
- "The grace of the Lord Jesus Christ and the love of God and the fellowship of the Holy Spirit be with you all" (2 Cor. 13:14).

Even though the Bible may describe him as spirit, wind, or fire, the Holy Spirit is a person. In the original Scripture languages, the Holy Spirit is referred to often with the masculine pronoun *he*—not the pronoun *it*. Consider John 16:13–14 as an example: "When the Spirit of truth comes, he will guide you into all the truth, for he will not speak on his own authority, but whatever he hears he will speak, and he will declare to you the things that are to come. He will glorify me, for he will take what is mine and declare it to you."

The Spirit is the part of God who is with us, teaching us and guiding us from within. We are the temple for the Holy Spirit as it says in 1 Corinthians 6:19: "Or do you not know that your body is a temple of the Holy Spirit within you, whom you have from God? You are not your own."

We hear him in our consciousness; he is that "gut" feeling telling us what is right or wrong. He can be that inner "ping" that lets you know to pay attention. The Holy Spirit helps us discern what is true and untrue. He is the voice of truth in our minds, that inner pull toward truth. He is the helper who guides us to the truth of Jesus Christ, for only through Jesus can we come to the Father. The three—the Holy Spirit, Jesus, and the Father—work together so that we can know the fullness of God and God's love for us.

Jesus tried to explain the importance of the Spirit to his disciples before he left this world. He knew they would need a helper and a guide: "If you love me, you will keep my commandments. And I will ask the Father, and he will give you another Helper, to be with you forever, even the Spirit of truth, whom the world cannot receive, because it neither sees him nor knows him. You know him, for he dwells with you and will be in you" (John 14:15–17).

I love how Carlo Carretto puts it. First I'll paraphrase: the Holy Spirit is the same love that unites the Father and the Son, he is the joy and fullness of God. Now, I give you the complete quote:

> The revelation of a triune God in the unity of a single nature, the revelation of a divine Holy Spirit present in us, is not on the human level; it does not belong to the realm of reason. It is a personal communication which God alone can give, and the task of giving it belongs to the Holy Spirit, who is the same love which unites the Father and Son. The Holy Spirit is the fullness and the joy of God.[15]

The Holy Spirit speaks to our hearts and reveals what the Father wills. He will teach us and help us to pray when we don't know what to pray: "Likewise the Spirit helps us in our weakness. For we do not know what to pray for as we ought, but the Spirit himself intercedes for us with groanings too deep for words" (Rom. 8:26).

The Holy Spirit will even help us to remember what we are being taught and what has been said to us through Jesus in the Bible: "But the Helper, the Holy Spirit, whom the Father will send in my name, he will teach you all things and bring to your remembrance all that I have said to you" (John 14:26).

If you haven't invited the Holy Spirit to come into your life, this is something to consider right now. Yes, he comes with Jesus, but recognizing him and specifically inviting him to change you is something extraordinary. Truly, as we learn in Matthew 3:11, the Holy Spirit is full of power. John alludes to this as he teaches people in the wilderness: "I baptize you with water for repentance, but he who is coming after me is mightier than I, whose sandals I am not worthy to carry. He will baptize you with the Holy Spirit and fire."

The baptism of Christ is both water and fire (Matt.3:11), yet somehow, we can miss the fire if we stop with repentance alone. Though repentance is a crucial step, recognizing the Holy Spirit as a separate but important part of the Holy Trinity and inviting him into your life is no small thing. Consider Paul's words to some of the early disciples in Ephesus:

> And he said to them, "Did you receive the Holy Spirit when you believed?" And they said, "No, we have not even heard that there is a Holy Spirit." And he said, "Into what then were you baptized?" They said, "Into John's baptism." And Paul said, "John baptized with the baptism of repentance, telling the people to believe in the one who was to come after him, that is, Jesus." On hearing this, they were baptized in the

> name of the Lord Jesus. And when Paul had laid his hands on them, the Holy Spirit came on them, and they began speaking in tongues and prophesying (Acts 19:2–6).

One simple prayer to invite the Holy Spirit into your life in a bigger way could be, "Holy Spirit, I praise you and recognize you as a person of the Holy Trinity. I have asked Jesus into my heart, but I also invite you to come into my life and baptize me in fire. Thank you for being with me and guiding me. In Jesus' name. Amen.

The one, mighty triune God created us to be a loving family under his patronage. Though he is mighty and strong and able to do all things, he wants us as his children, for he delights in us. He delights in you specifically, and there is a lot of proof of this in God's Word. We'll study what Scripture says about you in the next chapter.

Testimony on the Holy Spirit

The Holy Spirit was illusive for most of my upbringing. Perhaps you were given a better understanding, but I only remember him being described as wind, fire, or spirit, all of which were intangible and difficult for me to understand as a young person. But later in life I had an experience that helped clarify this matter.

Once I was sitting outside in my backyard, watching the leaves blowing in the breeze. I thought about how the only reason I knew there was a breeze was because the leaves were moving. Isn't that an interesting way to think of the Holy Spirit?

We cannot see him, but we know he is there when we see things around us moving.

When I asked the Holy Spirit into my life specifically and for the baptism of fire, I felt like a light switch had turned on inside me. All the sudden, I went from a place of darkness to light. I cannot explain it to you, but I saw things move in my life like never before. I saw the Word of God in the Bible with new eyes and heard God's voice in my conscience in greater ways. He is truly a person, with us and guiding us.

I pray you will receive the power of this third person of the Holy Trinity and that you would experience the fullness of God in your life. Amen.

Chapter 7
THE WORD FOR US: WHAT DOES GOD SAY ABOUT YOU?

O Lord, you have searched me and known me! You know when I sit down and when I rise up; you discern my thoughts from afar. You search out my path and my lying down and are acquainted with all my ways.

—Psalm 139:1–3

Why does God love us? What is it about us that is so important that he would give his only Son to see us returned to him? Believe it or not, God is madly in love with us and seeks our return. Just as the father in the parable of the prodigal son did not care about what the son did to squander his inheritance but welcomed him with open arms, our Father in heaven is seeking us and ready to forgive our past mistakes (Luke 15:11–32).

In the Bible, God says we are loved and are his beloved, his children, his workmanship. If ever you doubt your identity or hear negative self-talk in your mind, refer to Scripture and be reminded of who you are to him. God is waiting to hear from you. In fact, he longs to hear from you. He died so that you would be able to return to him. No matter what might have happened in our lives or what we've done, God's love is more than enough for our sins and our weakness.

Read the Scripture verses below to see what the Word of God says about you:

- **We are children of God:** "Yet to all who did receive him, to those who believed in his name, he gave the right to become children of God" (John 1:12, NIV).
- **We are adopted sons and daughters**: "He predestined us for adoption as sons through Jesus Christ, according to the purpose of his will" (Eph. 1:5).
- **We are no longer slaves to sin**: "We know that our old self was crucified with him in order that the body of sin might be brought to nothing, so that we would no longer be enslaved to sin" (Rom. 6:6).
- **We are made in his image:** "So God created man in his own image, in the image of God he created him; male and female he created them" (Gen. 1:27).
- **We are a chosen, royal priesthood**: "But you are a chosen people, a royal priesthood, a holy nation, God's special possession, that you may declare praises of him who called you out of darkness into his wonderful light" (1 Pet. 2:9, NIV).
- **We are his temple:** "Or do you not know that your body is a temple of the Holy Spirit within you, whom you have from God? You are not your own" (1 Cor. 6:19).

- **We are children of God and will be like him:** "See what kind of love the Father has given to us, that we should be called children of God; and so we are. The reason why the world does not know us is that it did not know him. Beloved, we are God's children now, and what we will be has not yet appeared; but we know that when he appears we shall be like him, because we shall see him as he is" (1 John 3:1–2).
- **We are hidden in Christ:** "For you died and your life is now hidden with Christ in God" (Col. 3:3, NIV).
- **We are a new creation**: "Therefore, if anyone is in Christ, he is a new creation. The old has passed away; behold, the new has come" (2 Cor. 5:17).
- **We are his workmanship**: "For we are his workmanship, created in Christ Jesus for good works which God prepared beforehand that we should walk in them" (Eph. 2:10).
- **We are the body of Christ:** "Now you are the body of Christ and individually members of it" (1 Cor. 12:27).
- **We are Abraham's offspring and heirs to the promise:** "And if you are Christ's then you are Abraham's offspring, heirs according to promise" (Gal. 3:29).
- **We are the branches who bear fruit:** "I am the vine; you are the branches. Whoever abides in me and I in him, he it is that bears much fruit, for apart from me you can do nothing" (John 15:5).
- **We are friends of Jesus:** "No longer do I call you servants, for the servant does not know what his master is doing; but I have called you friends, for all that I

have heard from my Father I have made known to you" (John 15:15).

- **We are redeemed and belong to him:** "But now thus says the LORD, he who created you, O Jacob, he who formed you, O Israel: "Fear not, for I have redeemed you; I have called you by name, you are mine" (Isa. 43:1).
- **We are clay, shaped by the hands of God:** "But now, O LORD, you are our Father; we are the clay, and you are our potter; we are all the work of your hand" (Isa. 64:8).
- **We are anointed and have his seal:** "And it is God who establishes us with you in Christ, and has anointed us, and who has also put his seal on us and given us his Spirit in our hearts as a guarantee" (2 Cor. 1:21–22).
- **We are now alive with Christ, saved and seated in heavenly places:** "But God, being rich in mercy, because of the great love with which he loved us, even when we were dead in our trespasses, made us alive together with Christ—by grace you have been saved and raised us up with him and seated us with him in the heavenly places in Christ Jesus" (Eph. 2:4–6).
- **We are his sheep, and he looks after us:** "For he is our God, and we are the people of his pasture, and the sheep of his hand. Today, if you hear his voice" (Ps. 95:7).
- **We are free from sin and death:** "There is therefore now no condemnation for those who are in Christ Jesus. For the law of the Spirit of life has set you

free in Christ Jesus from the law of sin and death" (Rom. 8:1–2).

- **We are co-crucified with Jesus:** "And those who belong to Christ Jesus have crucified the flesh with its passions and desires" (Gal. 5:24).
- **We are crowned with glory and honor:** "Yet you have made him a little lower than the heavenly beings and crowned him with glory and honor. You have given him dominion over the works of your hands; you have put all things under his feet" (Ps. 8:5–6).

This is only a sampling of what the Bible says about God and who we are to him. He is a loving God, ever working for our good, though he and his ways are higher than we can imagine. This God of amazing love and grace looks to us as his children, made in his image, and he crowns us with glory and honor. This is the God we seek to know more of through prayer. It is through prayer that our hearts can get in touch with God's heart. Jesus came to save us, and we can still give our heart to him today.

Testimony on Identity in God

I don't know about you, but I got stuck in my teen years, which were a time of darkness and confusion for me. I was left with all kinds of uncertainties about who I was and what my purpose should be. No one was ever extremely cruel to me. I wasn't frequently bullied as I stayed under the radar, but I was still a very shy and sensitive teenager.

As I grew up, I shed some of this old thinking, but I could never lose the thoughts of self-hatred, poor self-esteem, and lack of self-worth that I had picked up in my teens. Eventually God helped me realize that I had grown up believing the lie that I had been a mistake.

As an adoptee, my story was a common one. My birth parents were too young and had me out of wedlock, so I was put up for adoption. Somehow growing up, I misinterpreted these facts to mean I was a mistake. This was the root of many of the self-worth issues I had in childhood.

One day a new thought came into my mind: *What if your birthparents were brought together just to make you?* Now that is a thought worth keeping. (We'll talk more about discerning God's voice in chapter 13).

In this situation, truth set me free giving me a higher perspective. And I pray that the truth about who you are to God, based on the verses we've read together and others in the Bible, will help you realize your priceless value to God, our King.

Chapter 8

THE HEART OF THE MATTER: WHAT IS THE HEART, AND WHY IS IT IMPORTANT?

Think as little as possible about external ascetic feats. Although they are necessary, they are nothing but a scaffolding inside which the building is erected. They are not the building itself; the building is in the heart. Turn all your attention, then, on what is to be done in the heart.

—Theophan the Recluse

The heart is the seat of our inner being. It's the most precious part of who we are. Therefore, the heart is where Jesus desires to make his home in us. And we can make a home in his heart too.

The heart is where Jesus can reign supreme. It's more than feelings, more than emotions; the heart is our unique self that feels and senses, driving our will and our actions and colors our thoughts. Even the words we speak originate in our heart: "But what comes out of the mouth proceeds from the heart, and this defiles a person. For out of the heart come evil thoughts, murder, adultery, sexual immorality, theft, false witness, slander. These are what defile a person. But to eat with unwashed hands does not defile anyone" (Matt. 15:18–20).

Our actions prove our heart, as Abraham Joshua Heschell notes in his work, *God in Search of Man*: "God asks for the heart, but the heart is oppressed with uncertainty in its own twilight. God asks for faith, and the heart is not sure of its own faith. It is good that there is a dawn of decision for the sight of the heart; deeds to objectify faith, definitive forms to verify belief."[16]

Our hearts are meant to be one with God's heart, and prayer is a way to get closer to this original design. Paul writes in Romans 6:11, "So let it be the same way with you! Since you are now joined with him, you must continually view yourselves as dead and unresponsive to sin's appeal while living daily for God's pleasure in union with Jesus, the Anointed one" (TPT). As we receive Christ, we are joined in a holy union, a holy covenant with him where our hearts are joined as one.

This is the desire of our God: to have our heart joined as one heart with his. This is not always easy to do because the world is a difficult place; many of us have had our hearts broken and have thus built walls of protection around them. Fortunately, through prayer and God's grace, his love can transform us and bring the freedom and healing that come from God alone.

Why Is the Heart Important?

Through prayer we gain a heart of compassion, which allows us to see our fellow man in love and lead others out of confusion to clarification, as Nouwen notes below:

> For a man of prayer is, in the final analysis, the man who is able to recognize in others the face of the Messiah and make visible what was hidden, make touchable what was unreachable. The man of prayer is a leader precisely because through his articulation of God's work within himself he can lead others out of confusion to clarification; through his compassion he can guide them out of the closed circuits of their in-groups to the wide world of humanity; and through his critical contemplation he can convert their convulsive destructiveness into creative work for the new world to come.[17]

Though compassion and leading others to truth is crucial, Jesus wants to give believers even more. He came for our hearts because it is the place of our intentions and love; it's where he wants to reside.

Jesus did not come to live in our minds; that is not what the Bible says. Scriptures say that God *is* love, and he *is* love. It is in our hearts that love (aka God) can live, for that is where we experience love—not from the mind, from intellect and reason. No, love is in the heart. Thus, Paul prayed that Christ would dwell in the hearts of Ephesian believers: "I pray that from his glorious, unlimited resources he will empower you with inner strength through his Spirit. Then Christ will make his home in your hearts as you trust in him. Your roots will grow down into God's love and keep you strong" (Eph. 3:16–17, NLT).

The mind is not a bad thing, for it was created by God. However, if we are led by love (aka God) and the place love (God) resides is in our heart, then it would make sense that we are to be led by our hearts. This doesn't mean we should live from the place of our feelings, but if our hearts let Jesus in and Jesus rules in our hearts, then he will transform us into his likeness as he moderates and cares for our hearts, leading us in what is righteous. In this way, love can reign over our minds in righteousness and goodness. Letting love reign over our minds helps us to forgive others, live free from offense, and give when reason would say we shouldn't. The heart is a very important place, and Jesus knows this well. After all, he created our hearts and knows our hearts: "Then hear in heaven your dwelling place and forgive and act and render to each whose heart you know, according to all his ways (for you, you only, know the hearts of all the children of mankind)" (1 Kings 8:39).

God is so careful with our hearts. He searches our hearts, tests our minds, and sees not as we see but into the true heart of the individual: "I the Lord search the heart and test the mind, to give every man according to his ways, according to the fruit of his deeds" (Jer. 17:10).

He desires for us to have pure hearts, and Jesus preached on this in the Sermon on the Mount: "Blessed are the pure in heart, for they shall see God" (Matt. 5:8). We may at times build walls around our hearts, closing them off in a protected stance. But God knows what our hearts need and can communicate that to us through prayer. Listening to what God says we need is part of having an honest conversation with God. We'll discuss this more in chapter 12.

God looks at our hearts to prove our desires and to test our intentions: "But just as we have been approved by God to be entrusted with the gospel, so we speak, not to please man, but to please God who tests our hearts" (1 Thess. 2:4). Don't be surprised if he reveals some of your intentions as not pure or righteous. But know that if he does reveal things about your heart, he is full of grace and mercy. He only reveals darkness so that he may bring his healing light. Because, through it all, he desires for all to have salvation:

> And what is God's "living message"? It is the revelation of faith for salvation, which is the message that we preach. For if you publicly declare with your mouth that Jesus is Lord and believe in your heart that God raised him from the dead, you will experience salvation. The heart that believes in him receives the gift of the righteousness of God—and then the mouth gives thanks to salvation. For the Scriptures encourage us with these words: "Everyone who believes in him will never be disappointed" (Rom. 10:9–11, TPT).

So, take care of your heart and let him in so that you will be transformed. Then you can be free to experience the joys of his salvation that come through Christ alone.

Testimony on the Heart

Most of my teen and adult life I lived afraid. I listened to lies and false words about my identity. For protection, I placed a metaphorical metal plate over my heart. I was afraid of success; I was afraid of failure; I was afraid of people; I was afraid of losing people; I was afraid of just about everything. All this fear led to me blocking or walling myself off to most relationships, dreams, feelings, and more. I closed the doors of my heart, which led to a kind of numbness.

I used to drink and smoke, and though not an alcoholic, I found drinking to be one of the few things that allowed some of these walls to come down so that I could feel alive. Drinking was freeing because it allowed some of my true self to surface, and I desperately wanted to be me but I constantly felt trapped.

Thankfully Jesus was after my heart and slowly worked with me to take my barriers down. He gently removed the metal plate over my heart by bringing the truth of who he is and who I am to the forefront. He took my heart of stone and made it into a heart of flesh (Ezek. 36:26), and I have not had a desire to drink or smoke ever since.

I pray God would gently open your heart to see the great value he has placed on it. I pray for you to be transformed into the trueness of your identity in Christ as he abides with you. Amen.

Part 2

PRACTICAL HEART-TO-HEART PRAYER

Chapter 9

PRAYING FROM THE HEART

But the Lord said to Samuel, "Do not look on his appearance or on the height of his stature, because I have rejected him. For the Lord sees not as man sees: man looks on the outward appearance, but the Lord looks on the heart."

—1 Samuel 16:7

Prayer is a heart-to-heart conversation with God. God sees differently than we do. As you've been reading, it is the heart he is after, not appearance or anything superficial. How can we be closer in our hearts to God? Through prayer.

Now that you understand some of the elements of God and prayer, how does one pray? There are many ways to pray, but I'd like to outline an approach that hits many of the key elements of forming a strong relationship with the Lord. Here are the components:

1. **Discipline**: Set aside time to devote your heart to prayer.

2. **Praise**: Align your heart through worship and thanksgiving.
3. **Honesty**: Open your heart through humility, repentance, and forgiveness.
4. **Experience**: Grow your heart through listening, discerning, and trusting.

Discipline. Discipline is necessary because prayer requires time and devotion. Thinking about prayer or desiring to pray will not make prayer happen. Setting aside time and making a heartfelt commitment to follow through are needed efforts.

Praise. Praise aligns the heart to God. It brings us into a mindset where we can set aside our own agendas and focus on him. We do this through worship and thanksgiving.

Honesty. If we are honest with God in prayer, we can humbly allow the Spirit to reveal our shortfalls, which will lead us to repentance and forgiveness.

Experience. Through experience, our hearts can grow with God as a true relationship is developed by listening, discerning, and cultivating trust through Scripture and what we hear in our hearts from the Spirit.

If these things are done in prayer, they will provide anyone with a solid foundation to grow in a relationship with God. Now all of these things do not need to be done all together all the time. Sometimes only worship or thanksgiving happens, or we offer up a quick "please forgive me" prayer.

Starting at all is the first step toward an active prayer life that can grow your relationship with God. As the relationship grows, you'll find yourself creating disciplines, praising God regularly, and being more honest in your prayers as your experience with God grows. Then **transformation** and **freedom** will come as you experience more of who he is. Like you'll see in the next section, having the discipline to make time for devoted prayer is a great step toward an active prayer life and growing closer to the God who created us and loves us.

Chapter 10

DISCIPLINE: SET ASIDE TIME TO DEVOTE YOUR HEART TO PRAYER

The truth is, we only learn to pray all the time everywhere after we have resolutely set about praying some of the time somewhere.

—John Dalrymple

As with any relationship, it takes time to build a prayer life that leads to greater intimacy with God. A recent study from Jeffrey Hall, a University of Kansas professor, says that it takes about fifty hours of time spent together to move a relationship from casual acquaintance to casual friend. It takes ninety or more hours of time together to move to friend status and more than two hundred hours to be a close friend.[18] How can we hope to have a relationship with God if we do not give him our time? How can we ever know him if we ignore his presence in our lives?

So, if you set aside time, how is this time to be spent? Reading the Word is one way, but the study of Scripture alone, without prayer, is not enough. Carlo Carretto writes how intellectual study for the sake of knowledge is not the true intent of Christ:

> But pretending to know the other just by studying him in books or photographs means remaining outside real knowledge, real mystery. Today, many persons who seek or study God do just that. They study him in books, make him an object of speculation, approach him from intellectual curiosity. With what result? The more we study, the more our ideas become confused; the more we get caught up in discussions, the farther we go from him. I think this is the nature of the crisis in the Church today; it is a crisis of prayer, it is a crisis of contemplation. Study is no longer the light of spirituality, and curiosity has taken the place of humility.[19]

Though study and reading about God is not a bad thing, if it replaces spending time *with* God, it can be. Imagine what you would do with a friend you wanted to know better. Would you invite someone for coffee or tea for five minutes while multitasking around the house as they sat at your table? Of course not! Instead, you'd schedule a good amount of time and ensure few interruptions so that you could truly catch up. This is the same way we should think about God.

If it takes fifty hours of time with someone to become a casual friend, it's going to take a while to build a relationship with God. But do not be discouraged. Start where you can. Maybe take a fifteen-minute walk at lunchtime to give thanks and listen to an audio version of Scripture or use your twenty-minute drive to work to praise him and speak honestly to him about what's on your heart. You don't have to be locked in a prayer closet to work on your relationship with God. Anywhere can work if you can be free to focus on him.

Start with what is realistic, but I would aim to give at least fifteen minutes of your time to God on a regular basis. Eventually, you may find you want at least an hour or more, but start where you can. As you'll find in the next chapter, it's important to commit to prayer with a heart of devotion out of love and loyalty.

Testimony on Time

Once I realized God was alive and well and living with me day to day, moment to moment, I could not wait to spend time with him. I read the Old Testament in the morning and the New Testament at night. Whenever I had time, I would read and journal my thoughts on what I read. I'd pray on a passage and then listen to discern what resonated with me.

This takes time, so I went at my own pace. When days were busy and I could not sit in silence, I would use the time I had while driving to praise God by singing worship music or to talk to him about what was on my mind, just as if he were in the passenger seat. It's incredibly wonderful to know that God is right there with you, caring for your needs and listening to your words. As I put my concerns before him, I found that answers to questions would pop up and good ideas come to me as directed by the Spirit.

Begin where you can but do start. Carve out time in your schedule because this is a date you cannot afford to miss.

Scriptures to Aid in Prayer

Meditating on Scripture or asking the Lord to guide you in understanding his Word can enrich your prayer life. Below are a few Scriptures regarding time:

- "For he says, 'In the time of my favor I heard you, and in the day of salvation I helped you.' I tell you, now is the time of God's favor, now is the day of salvation" (2 Cor. 6:2, NIV).
- "Come now, you who say, 'Today or tomorrow we will go into such and such a town and spend a year there and trade and make a profit'—yet you do not know what tomorrow will bring. What is your life? For you are a mist that appears for a little time and then vanishes. Instead you ought to say, 'If the Lord wills, we will live and do this or that'" (Jas. 4:13–15).
- "My times are in your hand; rescue me from the hand of my enemies and from my persecutors!" (Ps. 31:15).
- "Besides this you know the time, that the hour has come for you to wake from sleep. For salvation is nearer to us now than when we first believed" (Rom. 13:11).
- "The world and its desires pass away, but whoever does the will of God lives forever" (1 John 2:17, NIV).
- "He has made everything beautiful in its time. He has also set eternity in the human heart; yet no one can

fathom what God has done from beginning to end" (Eccles. 3:11, NIV).
- "The plans of the diligent lead to profit as surely as haste leads to poverty" (Prov. 21:5, NIV).

Devotion

> *[During prayer] If the heart wanders or is distracted, bring it back to the point quite gently and replace it tenderly in its Master's presence. And even if you did nothing during the whole of your hour but bring your heart back and place it again in Our Lord's presence, though it went away every time you brought it back, your hour would be very well employed.*
>
> —St. Francis de Sales

God loves us. That is the heart of devotion and the heart of prayer. Come to his table, for you are welcome. He is loving and kind and wants to be a part of your life. Taking time to talk to God in prayer is a joy, but in the beginning, it might not feel that way. I encourage you to come with thanksgiving as prayer is meant to be done out of love for God or a desire to learn to love him. It's not something on a checklist or a way to feel devout. A heart of prayer in pursuit of God is the pathway to devotion.

If you want to develop a prayer life, be dedicated; make it a discipline, not a chore. And as the quote above by St. Francis de Sales indicates, even if you spend the whole time trying to focus, you have achieved much. It is important to take a first step.

The *Lexicon Online Dictionary* defines *devotion* as religious worship or observance.[20] An *observance* is the action or practice of fulfilling or respecting the requirements of law, morality, or ritual.[21] This definition alludes to action; we are doing something related to our beliefs or morals. Examples of practicing devotion include creating a routine that carves out time with God, doing an activity that involves reading Scripture, or simply resting in what God is doing in your life. Though not included in this definition, for purposes of prayer, whatever you do in devotion must be done with a heart or desire to pursue God, to know him, and to love him. If this is hard, worship and praise are great ways to prepare yourself. We'll talk more about worship and praise in chapter 11.

To take some practical steps, consider making a schedule or routine. For example, spend every lunch hour in a quiet place with God or set aside time to be with him before bedtime or every morning. Depending on your lifestyle and schedule, you can find room to fit God into the day. Utilizing the steps we discuss in the next chapters will help you use this time well.

In some cases, it may feel forced. And if it's not your normal routine, it may even be challenging. This quote by St. John Kronstadt describes the journey of prayer: "Learn to pray; force yourself to prayer. In the beginning it will be difficult, but afterwards the more you force yourself to pray, the more easily you will do so."

But like anything new, it will become more and more comfortable as you lean into the presence of the Lord in your prayer time. You may even feel like it's the best part of your day.

Whatever routine you decide on for prayer, stick with it for at least twenty-one days as that's about how long it takes to form a new habit, according to cognitive neuroscientist Dr. Caroline Leaf.[22] Over time, you will see improvement and an increase in ease in making the time and effort to be alone with God.

As you pray, do not lose heart. In fact, Jesus shared a parable with the disciples to give them hope as they prayed:

> And he told them a parable to the effect that they ought always to pray and not lose heart. He said, "In a certain city there was a judge who neither feared God nor respected man. And there was a widow in that city who kept coming to him and saying, 'Give me justice against my adversary.' For a while he refused, but afterward he said to himself, 'Though I neither fear God nor respect man, yet because this widow keeps bothering me, I will give her justice, so that she will not beat me down by her continual coming.'" And the Lord said, "Hear what the unrighteous judge says. And will not God give justice to his elect, who cry to him day and night? Will he delay long over them? I tell you, he will give justice to them speedily. Nevertheless, when the Son of Man comes, will he find faith on earth?" (Luke 18:1–8).

Let these verses encourage you. If even a judge who did not fear God nor man would listen to the persistent widow, how much more will God listen to the prayers of his children as they cry out repeatedly to him? Our God is one who hears what we say. Make no mistake. His Word is true, and he will respond, but we need to be paying attention.

As you pray, be encouraged. Remember who God is and what he says about you. It is almost like a courtship, for God would woo each of us to his side in his intense love for us. Therefore, he is worthy of our devotion and a lifetime of pursuit.

We'll address ways to talk to God and what you can do during your prayer time in the following chapters.

Practical Tip

It's good to be intentional with your prayer time and to pay attention to how you prepare yourself. Charles Swindoll says there are actually four disciplines to cultivating intimacy with God.[23] I think we can apply these to prayer. These disciplines are repeated actions that cultivate a lifestyle and help you achieve your goal:

1. Simplicity: to reorder one's private world
2. Silence: to be still
3. Solitude: to cultivate serenity
4. Surrender: to trust the Lord completely

I'd like to share my takeaways for each of these disciplines:

1. Simplicity: Our lives are busy, and things can get complicated; so, remove the clutter in your schedule and in your mind so you can simply sit before the Lord.
2. Silence: To hear his voice, you need silence, a break from the noise and distractions of the world.

3. Solitude: Spending time alone reflecting gives you time to process what you are hearing and learning.
4. Surrender: Trusting God enough to leave your future and life in his hands is an act of obedience from a heart of love.

Following these four steps is one way to prepare your heart for devotion to the Lord in prayer. Decluttering your mind will help you focus on God. If silence isn't for you, ask yourself why. Do you fear inactivity because you've tied your worth to work or busyness? Sit with the Lord or talk to a trusted friend to see if you can uncover any hidden motives that keep you from finding that inner stillness. If finding solitude is difficult, start by prioritizing a personal break of fifteen minutes. Or give yourself time to do one of your favorite activities or pastimes alone and spend it talking to God. Even working in the garden by yourself is a great time to talk to the Lord. Surrender can be difficult and is a matter of trust. We'll talk more about trust in chapter 13.

Testimony on Devotion

With the Holy Spirit in my life, God has never been more real. He is like a person to me. Jesus called himself the Son of Man, and he is also fully God. I want to give him everything, knowing what he's given me. I desire deep intimacy with him, but cannot, of course, do it on my own, and it could never have been done the way I was living when he came into my life.

He worked on my heart, and as I gave him time, I learned about who he was in the Bible and devoted myself to learning of his love. Previously, I had protected my heart and kept many people out—including God. I did not know his love because I hid behind a wall. But God can do all things, so he broke down my wall and taught me about his goodness and kindness. He gave me his perspective on things that had bothered me for years.

All the reading, journaling, worship, and sermons—all the things that came before me to teach me about God—these things were all from a heart of devotion to know him more. I had a deep hunger for him that only grew as I learned more. As Jeremiah 29:13 says, "You will seek me and find me, when you seek me with all your heart." I was a seeker, and he was faithful to help me find him through his Word, teachings, prayer, and the Holy Spirit.

I pray that this same desire comes over you as you ask God into your life and seek him with all your heart.

Scriptures to Aid in Prayer

Meditating on Scripture and asking the Lord to guide you in the understanding of his Word can enrich your prayer life. Below are a few Scriptures regarding devotion:

- "Commit your work to the Lord, and your plans will be established" (Prov. 16:3).
- "All Scripture is breathed out by God and profitable for teaching, for reproof, for correction, and for training in

righteousness, that the man of God may be competent, equipped for every good work" (2 Tim. 3:16–17).

- "Finally, brothers, whatever is true, whatever is honorable, whatever is just, whatever is pure, whatever is lovely, whatever is commendable, if there is any excellence, if there is anything worthy of praise, think about these things. What you have learned and received and heard and seen in me—practice these things, and the God of peace will be with you" (Phil. 4:8–9).
- "Put on then, as God's chosen ones, holy and beloved, compassionate hearts, kindness, humility, meekness, and patience" (Col. 3:12).
- "No servant can serve two masters, for either he will hate the one and love the other, or he will be devoted to the one and despise the other. You cannot serve God and money" (Luke 16:13).
- "If then you have been raised with Christ, seek the things that are above, where Christ is, seated at the right hand of God" (Col. 3:1).
- "Beware of practicing your righteousness before other people in order to be seen by them, for then you will have no reward from your Father who is in heaven"(Matt. 6:1).

Chapter 11

PRAISE: ALIGN YOUR HEART THROUGH WORSHIP AND THANKSGIVING

It is a wonderfully blessed thing to be privileged to share together the common mood of worship. Miraculous indeed is it to mingle the individual life with its intensely private quality in a transcendent moment of synthesis and fusion—here it is that the uniquely personal is lifted up and seen in a perspective as broad as life, and as profound! [24]

—Howard Thurman, *The Inward Journey*

Aligning our hearts through praise and worship will allow us to transcend our own thoughts and worries to reach another place of being with God. Sometimes in worship, it can feel like we have left earth for a spiritual dimension, as Paul describes in Ephesians 2:6: "And God raised us up with Christ and seated us with him in the heavenly realms in Christ Jesus" (NIV).

In worship we can resound with heaven's praise. What does it mean to *resound*? Let's consider the word *resonance*, which is a scientific term. If you take a tuning fork tuned at the same frequency as another and strike it, it will start vibrating. The other tuning fork, set to the same pitch, will also vibrate, though it hasn't been struck. This means it "resounds." In worship, our heart gets tuned to the same pitch as God's heart, and we tune to his frequency or presence. The psalmist understood the resonance creation can have with the Creator: "Say among the nations, 'The LORD reigns.' The world is firmly established, it cannot be moved; he will judge the peoples with equity. Let the heavens rejoice, let the earth be glad; let the sea resound, and all that is in it" (Ps. 96:10–11, NIV).

In a lot of ways, prayer and worship are married. Worship prepares our hearts to be in his presence, removing our self-focus and drawing our hearts toward his magnificent power and grace. Then prayer can be focused and free of any clutter in our hearts. Prayer and worship pair together well and strengthen each other by aligning our hearts with the heart of God, thus paving the way for us to be in his mighty presence.

Worship does not have to be song. It can come in many forms, often related to the arts, like dancing, painting, and poetry. Art allows creative forms of expression that can bring God into focus and allow us to lose ourselves in his presence. Paul encouraged the Ephesians to encounter God through song: "Speaking to one another with psalms, hymns, and songs from the Spirit. Sing and make music from your heart to the Lord, always giving thanks to God the Father for everything, in the name of our Lord Jesus Christ" (Eph. 5:19–20, NIV).

As was true at Jericho, worship can also be a powerful weapon against the enemy. As we read in Joshua 6, Joshua is instructed by God to command Israel to march around the city walls of Jericho and, at the appointed time, sound their trumpets and raise a great shout to the Lord. At that time, Joshua is told, the walls will come down, and the city will be theirs for the taking.

Now, because of the sacrifice of our Lord Jesus Christ, which atoned for our sins, we can still experience the triumphant power of praise and worship. Worship can still bring down the walls of the enemy—just as it did in this ancient story—to release God's blessing in our lives.

King David was near to the heart of God because he was always praising God and seeking his ways. Not only was he the King of Israel and a mighty warrior, but he was also an accomplished worship leader, writing music and playing his lyre for King Saul and others.

David poured out his heart to God in psalms, and the book of Psalms is a good place to look for examples of worship and prayer. The chapters in Psalms are full of emotion, many written by David, who was at war or hiding from Saul and seeking God's guidance and comfort. With a heart of worship and praise, David finds his confidence in the Lord, even when afraid or downcast:

> The LORD is my light and my salvation—whom shall I fear? The LORD is the stronghold of my life—of whom shall I be afraid? When the wicked advance

> against me to devour me, it is my enemies and my foes who will stumble and fall. Though an army besiege me, my heart will not fear; though war break out against me, even then I will be confident (Ps. 27:1–3).

As you seek the Lord, turn on some worship music and meditate on these words from Psalm 27. Read a love poem or express your love for God through your own music. He loves to hear us pour out our praises to him in a variety of ways. The longer you spend in worship, the more your heart can resonate with the heart of God. His presence can then come and settle on you to prepare your heart to speak to him in prayer.

Testimony on Worship

Days can be long and difficult, so it's not always easy to keep our eyes on God. When I get angry, confused, upset, or frustrated—all the things I don't want to be—it's a great time for me to put on worship music.

I had a difficult day when my husband and I had to put our dog down. It was one of the worst experiences of my life. But after crying out to God, I put on worship music and found that my heart was lifted out of the hard place to where I could focus on who God is to me. I was reminded that he is powerful and sovereign, that he cares for all the things in my life. This refocusing filled my soul with joy, and I was able to remember his goodness and his promise to bring healing to my heart and help me through times of sorrow and loss. Even through my tears I could praise him with a heart of gratitude as I was comforted by the songs' words of love.

I pray that you'll be reminded to worship God in your times of joy and struggle.

Scriptures to Aid in Prayer

Meditating on Scripture or asking the Lord to guide you in understanding his Word can enrich your prayer life. Below are a few Scriptures regarding worship:

- "Oh come, let us worship and bow down; let us kneel before the Lord, our Maker!" (Ps. 95:6).
- "Sing praises to the Lord, for he has done gloriously; let this be made known in all the earth" (Isa. 12:5).
- "But the hour is coming, and is now here, when the true worshipers will worship the Father in spirit and truth, for the Father is seeking such people to worship him" (John 4:23).
- "And above all these put on love, which binds everything together in perfect harmony. And let the peace of Christ rule in your hearts, to which indeed you were called in one body. And be thankful. Let the word of Christ dwell in you richly, teaching and admonishing one another in all wisdom, singing psalms and hymns and spiritual songs, with thankfulness in your hearts to God. And whatever you do, in word or deed, do everything in the name of the Lord Jesus, giving thanks to God the Father through him" (Col. 3:14–17).
- "And Jesus answered him, 'It is written, "You shall worship the Lord your God, and him only shall you serve"'" (Luke 4:8).

- "Ascribe to the Lord the glory due his name; worship the Lord in the splendor of holiness" (Ps. 29:2).

Thanksgiving

Shouts of joy and victory resound in the tents of the righteous: "The Lord's right hand has done mighty things! The Lord's right hand is lifted high; the Lord's right hand has done mighty things!"

—Psalm 118:15–16, NIV

Enter his gates with thanksgiving (Ps. 100:4). He deserves all our thanks, but the act of giving thanks also prepares our hearts to be in his presence. Thanksgiving aligns us with God's heart and turns our focus from ourselves to him.

Having a thankful heart is an antidote for many sins. Try to be jealous of someone if you are thankful for what you have—it's not possible. If you are truly thankful for God and what he has given you, coveting or being jealous will not plague you, nor will you get angry or upset about the difficulties in your life. Having a thankful heart is about setting aside what we want and all the cares of our day and saying, "Nothing is as important as God and his love and mercy for us."

Isn't that wonderful? What if we expressed our thanks out loud to our loved ones? Or what if someone you loved stopped everything and truly thanked you for what you mean to them? Wow, wouldn't that feel nice? It would make anyone feel loved. Isn't that the least we could do for such a good and loving God?

David understood what thanksgiving can do in a heart. He appointed a song or thanks to be sung publicly to celebrate bringing the Ark of the Covenant back into Israel's assembly: "Give thanks to the LORD, for he is good; his love endures forever" (1 Chron. 16:34, NIV). In Psalm 107:8–9, the psalmist encourages thanks for the deliverance the Lord gave his people: "Let them give thanks to the LORD for his unfailing love and his wonderful deeds for mankind, for he satisfies the thirsty and fills the hungry with good things" (NIV). Throughout the Bible, we see thanksgiving as an important element in the communication between God and man.

Thanksgiving may sound easy, but it can be challenging to feel thankful when we are struggling, worried, anxious, or facing difficulties. Hardship is real, and it is natural to feel upset, sad, or angry. However, if we can set the problems aside and think about the good things God has done, we can gain new perspective.

You may have heard the phrase, "sacrifice of praise" (Heb. 13:15), which means it can sometimes feel like a sacrifice to praise God in times of sorrow, anger, or fear. But God, in his immense love for us, knows our hearts and can use whatever is happening in our life for our good (Rom. 8:28). Turning our focus from our pain to God in gratitude can bring immense healing to our hearts.

Testimony of Thanksgiving

There is a famous hymn called, "It is Well With My Soul," by Horatio Spafford and Philip Bliss. I often think of this song when I am turning my heart toward praise and thanksgiving because it's hardest to "raise an hallelujah" when we are feeling sad, angry, or full of despair. When the world seems to be falling apart, thanking God is difficult. But remember, we only see in part; he sees the full picture (1 Cor. 13:9–12).

My husband and I were in the process of adopting our daughter when we were given the opportunity to adopt her biological sister as well. The money, the unknowns, and the uncertainty of adopting two, when we had not yet brought home one, were overwhelming. It was such a difficult decision. As an adoptee myself, I wanted with all of my heart to have a "blood-relative" sibling for my daughter. Yet I felt very clearly like our circumstances clearly hindered us from this possibility, and as I prayed, I felt that God himself was saying no as well.

At this point, I had to raise a hallelujah while thanking him for the opportunity and acknowledging that he knew best where this child should live and be raised. It was not an easy decision, but he has brought so much joy from it. This sibling was adopted by an amazing family in another state, but we are able to see them and enjoy time together through video calls and visits. Now we have not just a sibling in America for our daughter but an entire family she is now linked with through her biological sister.

God saved us too because I changed jobs shortly after our daughter came home, going from a high-paying, for-profit job to a lower paying, nonprofit job. We could not have afforded another child then, and God knew that. We only saw in part, and we are grateful that God knew what was best for all parties. May you be able to thank God in all your situations, whether good or challenging.

Scriptures to Aid in Prayer

Meditating on Scripture or asking the Lord to guide you in understanding his Word can enrich your prayer life. Below are a few Scriptures regarding thanksgiving:

- "Give thanks in all circumstances; for this is the will of God in Christ Jesus for you" (1 Thess. 5:18).
- "Oh, give thanks to the Lord, for he is good, for his steadfast love endures forever!" (Ps. 107:1).
- "Do not be anxious about anything, but in everything by prayer and supplication with thanksgiving let your requests be made known to God" (Phil. 4:6).
- "I will give to the Lord the thanks due to his righteousness, and I will sing praise to the name of the Lord, the Most High" (Ps. 7:17).
- "Giving thanks always and for everything to God the Father in the name of our Lord Jesus Christ" (Eph. 5:20).
- "Make a joyful noise to the Lord, all the earth! Serve the Lord with gladness! Come into his presence with singing! Know that the Lord, he is God! It is he who made us, and we are his; we are his people, and the sheep of his pasture. Enter his gates with thanksgiving, and his courts with praise! Give thanks to him; bless his name! For the Lord is good; his steadfast love endures forever, and his faithfulness to all generations" (Ps. 100:1–5).

- "Through him then let us continually offer up a sacrifice of praise to God, that is, the fruit of lips that acknowledge his name" (Heb. 13:15).

Chapter 12

HONESTY: OPEN YOUR HEART THROUGH HUMILITY, REPENTANCE, AND FORGIVENESS

Our spiritual life is his affair; because whatever we may think to the contrary, it is really produced by his steady attraction, and our humble and self-forgetful response to it. It consists in being drawn, at his pace and in his way, to the place he wants us to be; not the place we fancied for ourselves. [25]

—Evelyn Underhill, *The Spiritual Life*

Taking time in prayer to humbly look into your heart, to consider your feelings and what is going on inside of you, is an important part of prayer. When we are honest with God and ourselves, we arrive at truth, and truth sets us free (John 8:32).

A heart must be humble and repentant to confess sin and also recognize its own sinfulness to fully forgive others. It is not an easy process, but as we stand before a God who is loving, gentle, and mighty, we can rest assured that he is ready to forgive us.

To this purpose, a popular prayer model some find helpful uses the acronym ACTS to guide you through an honest examination of self in prayer. ACTS stands for adoration, confession, thanksgiving, and supplication. It uses some of the elements we already shared with you but adds confession and supplication.

- **Adoration:** Profess your love and appreciation to God. The psalms are full of adoration if you need examples. (Ps. 150, Rev. 4:11)
- **Confession:** Admit your sins and ask for forgiveness. (1 John 1:9)
- **Thanksgiving:** Thank him for all he has done or is doing in your life. (Ps. 100:4)
- **Supplication:** Make a request for yourself or others. (Phil. 4:6)

In the following sections, we'll go into more depth about what it means and what it takes to have humility, be repentant of your sin, and then forgive others with the same grace you've received. Through fully embracing these concepts, you can find transformation and freedom as you converse with God in your prayer time.

Humility

Throughout Psalms, we read of David praising God in every situation with a humble and contrite heart. He looks at his heart honestly and shares it with God. Through his recorded prayers, we can see his heart change from upset and afraid to humble and secure in God. David's pursuit of God in prayer earned him the description, "a man after God's own heart" (1 Sam. 13:13-14).

When you read David's psalms as examples of prayers, you see what it sounds like to pour out your heart without restraint to God. We can approach God in this way too. It's not about appeasing an angry God; it's not about duty. Prayer is connecting to the heart of God as you would connect with a dear friend or trusted family member. You can honestly share what is on your heart without pride or intimidation: "You will seek me and find me when you seek me with all your heart" (Jer. 29:13).

Think about turning to a dear friend or trusted family member for comfort or support. What kind of things do you share? Sometimes we share stories of our day and things we enjoyed; we may express gratitude or thanks. Other times, we share our troubles, our hurts, and our pain. This is true of how David talked to the Lord. He poured out his heart, and God drew close to David and there developed an intimate relationship. It's like the stages of prayer discussed at the beginning of this book. We can all have such a relationship if we are willing to open our hearts to God, not putting ourselves higher than he is but coming with a posture of love and humility. God will always love us but that kind of closeness is only developed through relationship, and that is a two-way street. God gives but we need to be a part of that equation. He cannot grow with us if we ignore him or deny his existence.

Look at Psalm 25:15–18, for example. David doesn't give up on loving God in hardship: "My eyes are ever toward the Lord, for he will pluck my feet out of the net. Turn to me and be gracious to me, for I am lonely and afflicted. The troubles of my heart are enlarged; bring me out of my distresses. Consider my affliction and my trouble, and forgive all my sins." David speaks directly to the Lord concerning his trouble, humbling himself and sharing his loneliness, pain, and distress. Even when he knew he had sinned, David still drew near to God and sought his neverending forgiveness.

Sorrow, joy, confession, thanksgiving—these are all good things to share with the Lord as he is ever eager to hear from us, help us, or listen to us. He is not judging or looking to punish; rather, in love, he longs to support us and guide us. No fancy words need to be said in prayer or conversation with God. You can be open and honest as you would talk to a friend.

In some cases, places in our lives may need discipline. Though it isn't always pleasant to experience, God disciplines us because he loves us. Even in discipline, he shows us grace, giving us more than we can ask or imagine:

> The first lesson God gives us in training our will is in making us go halfway with him. He first puts us through a series of disciplines to see if we are worthy to make his team. After his lesson is learned we discover that there are many, many times that God goes all the way with us. Over and over again he gives us far more than we have any right to ask. We call this, "his Grace," which goes so much farther than "his law" requires that he should go. God's mercy goes so much farther than mere human justice goes.[26]

If discipline leads to humility, we are very blessed, for humility is where we can find God's grace (Jas. 4:6). Having a humble heart saves us from pride, which comes before a fall (Prov. 16:18). And humility is a great protection for us as it leads to an open heart that allows us to grow. With humility, we can be repentant and forgiving as you'll read about in the following pages.

Testimony on Humility

I've seen great change in my life over the years as I've sought the Lord. For a long time, I was limited by my fear, doubt, and anxiety. During a season in my past, I worked for an organization that was predominately male. I did not always navigate these relationships well as a woman, nor did I understand the different perspective of my superiors. But one night I had a dream.

Dreams are significant as we learn in Acts 2:17: "'And in the last days it shall be, God declares, that I will pour out my Spirit on all flesh, and your sons and your daughters shall prophesy, and your young men shall see visions, and your old men shall dream dreams." Scriptures often speak of people having dreams. Now, that is not to say that all our dreams mean something or that we should be fixated on the interpretation of dreams. We must be careful to avoid falling into new age thinking or taking our eyes off God.

However, in this instance, I dreamed I was on a high horse, and I was nervous, knowing I could easily fall. As I woke, I thought this was a significant dream, as I remembered what it means to be "on a high horse." The connotation is not very complimentary.

So, I prayed about this and looked into my heart to ask myself, *Am I acting like someone on a figurative high horse?* Well, if I was being honest and humble about it, yes, I probably was. I checked with Scripture to see what it says about pride. If you look up verses on pride, it's easy to see that pride isn't good.

I realized I needed to humble myself, so I approached two men I was working with and apologized for acting like I was on a high horse. I repented, not wanting to continue such behavior. It was received with grace, as 1 Pet. 5:5 notes below, and it moved my heart to be more mindful of the way I acted and to check with my heart more often for signs of pride.

I pray the Lord will show you areas of your life that need humbling. Humility is a key characteristic of those in God's Kingdom, for it opens our hearts to receive correction and move forward with actions that bless us and those around us. As you'll see in the following Scriptures, great rewards accompany true humility. May you walk humbly with the Lord and those around you.

Scriptures to Aid in Prayer

Meditating on Scripture and asking the Lord to guide you in understanding his Word can enrich your prayer life. Below are a few Scriptures regarding humility before God and others:

- "The reward for humility and fear of the Lord is riches and honor and life" (Prov. 22:4).

- "Likewise, you who are younger, be subject to the elders. Clothe yourselves, all of you, with humility toward one another, for 'God opposes the proud but gives grace to the humble'" (1 Pet. 5:5).
- "Put on then, as God's chosen ones, holy and beloved, compassionate hearts, kindness, humility, meekness, and patience" (Col. 3:12).
- "But he gives more grace. Therefore it says, 'God opposes the proud, but gives grace to the humble'" (Jas. 4:6).
- "When pride comes, then comes disgrace, but with the humble is wisdom" (Prov. 11:2).
- "With all humility and gentleness, with patience, bearing with one another in love" (Eph. 4:2).
- "Humble yourselves before the Lord, and he will exalt you" (Jas. 4:10).
- "The fear of the Lord is instruction in wisdom, and humility comes before honor" (Prov. 15:33).
- "Do nothing from selfish ambition or conceit, but in humility count others more significant than yourselves" (Phil. 2:3).
- "For by the grace given to me I say to everyone among you not to think of himself more highly than he ought to think, but to think with sober judgment, each according to the measure of faith that God has assigned" (Rom. 12:3).
- "Toward the scorners he is scornful, but to the humble he gives favor" (Prov. 3:34).

- "If my people who are called by my name humble themselves, and pray and seek my face and turn from their wicked ways, then I will hear from heaven and will forgive their sin and heal their land" (2 Chron. 7:14).

Repentance

Repent, then, and turn to God, so that your sins may be wiped out, that times of refreshing may come from the Lord.
—Acts 3:19, NIV

When worship and thanksgiving have aligned your heart to the Lord and you are open to his ways, you can lay down before him the areas of your life that do not honor him. This is an important part of keeping a healthy relationship with God and can be transformative as we grow in our relationship with Christ.

To *repent*, as defined by *Merriam-Webster*, means "to turn from sin and dedicate oneself to the amendment of one's life."[27] It is turning away from something we have done or are doing that we know to be wrong and instead dedicating ourselves to doing what God says is right.

To understand repentance, it is helpful to understand the concepts of sin, iniquity, and transgression, all of which are mentioned in the Bible as hinderances to a deeper relationship with God and a connected prayer life.

Sin means to miss the mark.[28] It is doing anything not in line with God's righteousness. David knew the importance of owning his sins as we see in Psalm 32:5: "Then I acknowledged my sin to you and did not cover up my iniquity. I said, 'I will confess my transgressions to the Lord.' And you forgave the guilt of my sin" (NIV).

Iniquity is a gross injustice or wickedness.[29] A synonym is *corruption*. Iniquity tends to be more rooted in the intention of the action or the heart's attitude towards a situation.

Transgression is to infringe or go beyond the bounds of (a moral principle or other established standard of behavior).[30] A synonym is *misbehavior*. A transgression occurs when one avoids following law or rules. A transgressor has a rebellious nature.

Why do these three words matter? Each of them addresses something we can search our hearts for and bring before the Lord. Did we miss the mark (sin) in some way, knowing that God would want us to do it differently?

Did we have the right heart when we did something? We can certainly do what is right but with a wrong heart, which can lead to an iniquity. For example, a child can obey his parent's request to make his bed but with a lot of huffing and puffing. No, this isn't a gross iniquity, but it demonstrates our heart's posture. The Bible says to do all things for the glory of God—all things.

Did we do something we knew was wrong but still did it anyway (transgression)? Taking something from the store without paying, from someone we know without asking, or from our workplace that belongs to the office isn't right. In this example, transgression is when we think we are superior to others or deserve something we did not earn and take it for ourselves.

No one is above any of these things. We have all sinned and fallen short of the glory of God (Rom. 3:23). However, if we repent and turn to God, he will wash away our sins, and we can begin again with a clean slate. In 1 John 1:9, we are promised, "If we confess our sins, he is faithful and just to forgive us our sins and to cleanse us from all unrighteousness".

We miss the truth of who we are made to be when we sin. When we confess our sins, we are forgiven because his death, his blood sacrifice, paid the debt for what we have done. True repentance comes from the heart and can motivate us to change the actions that needed forgiveness to actions of righteousness and love.

Jesus' forgiveness has no limits. His blood is sufficient. Jesus explains this kind of boundless forgiveness in Matthew 18:21–22 (NLT) when Peter asks how many times we should forgive our neighbor. Jesus says seventy times seven, which implies an infinite amount of grace for those who transgress. But when we repent, there should be sincere remorse and a dedication to truly turn one's life around. We are actually commanded to repent in Acts 17:30: "In the past God overlooked such ignorance, but now he commands all people everywhere to repent" (NIV).

Repentance opens our hearts so we can first be honest about our sin nature and then be cleansed in his presence. If we live our lives without repentance, it is much like going to the same bathroom over and over but without flushing the toilet. Ever been in one of those gas station restrooms that hasn't been cleaned in a week or two? It's not pretty. This is what our hearts can look like if we are not regularly cleansing them through repentance. The buildup of sin, iniquity and transgressions can cause issues in our relationships or lead to patterns of thought and action that prohibit us from being our best. Our unconfessed sins create not only a mess for us but also a mess for others to be around. Who wants to live in that kind of state?

As we see some of this mess in ourselves, we might want to turn and run away, but I want to encourage you by reminding you that you are not alone in cleaning this mess. God gave us a helper, the Holy Spirit, who is present with us to guide us in these things. If we choose, he will help us begin the laborious process of mopping the floor, scrubbing the walls, and so on. Through repentance, forgiveness, and humility, you may soon find things looking better. After entering deep inner work with God, you will see the bathroom's beautiful handmade Italian tile unfold with its intricate patterns of colors and shapes.

By repenting of your sins, iniquities, and transgressions, the truth of who you are as a beautiful, unique child of God can be revealed. He desires this process for us all: "The Lord is not slow in keeping his promise, as some understand slowness. Instead he is patient with you, not wanting anyone to perish, but everyone to come to repentance" (2 Pet. 3:9, NIV).

Testimony of Repentance

It's funny being a parent sometimes because our children often mirror us. I found that as I raised my daughter, I would see things she'd do and say, and think, *Wait, do I do that?* In some cases, it was cute; in others, it wasn't so pretty.

One day, I noticed she was criticizing her father and bossing him around. For example, she said, "Daddy, you should do the dishes because you never do the dishes." She'd look at me, expecting me to be pleased that she had followed my example.

But I sat horrified, realizing she was copying me. My heart, feeling neglected by my husband, took it out on him through criticism and poisonous words. I had set this example for my daughter.

I am not proud of this story, but I share it because it convicted me to seek the Lord and ask him why I was critical and what I could do about it. First, I had to repent to God in prayer for the way I had behaved. I had to forgive my husband for any grievances I held against him, whether true or untrue. I looked to the Bible, searching for what it said about wives; I found I was sorely lacking. I devoted my prayer time to asking the Lord for help overcoming this terrible behavior. He heard me and indeed helped.

Through prayer, study, wise counsel, and Scripture, I changed my perspective. I had to live from a place of knowing my husband loved me. And I needed to express my love for him in ways that were positive. I had to learn to talk to my husband about areas in which I felt neglected and come up with positive ways to remedy these grievances, without accusation. It took time, but with God's leading at every step, I have a much healthier relationship with my husband, and my daughter can now learn what love looks like from her parents.

Scriptures to Aid in Prayer

Meditating on Scripture or asking the Lord to guide you in understanding his Word can enrich your prayer life. Below are a few Scriptures regarding repentance:

- "Just so, I tell you, there will be more joy in heaven over one sinner who repents than over ninety-nine righteous persons who need no repentance" (Luke 15:7).
- "The Lord is not slow to fulfill his promise as some count slowness, but is patient toward you, not wishing that any should perish, but that all should reach repentance" (2 Pet. 3:9).
- "From that time Jesus began to preach, saying, 'Repent, for the Kingdom of heaven is at hand'" (Matt. 4:17).
- "And Peter said to them, "Repent and be baptized every one of you in the name of Jesus Christ for the forgiveness of your sins, and you will receive the gift of the Holy Spirit" (Acts 2:38).
- "The times of ignorance God overlooked, but now he commands all people everywhere to repent" (Acts 17:30).
- "I have not come to call the righteous but sinners to repentance" (Luke 5:32).
- "Those whom I love, I reprove and discipline, so be zealous and repent" (Rev. 3:19).
- "For godly grief produces a repentance that leads to salvation without regret, whereas worldly grief produces death" (2 Cor. 7:10).
- "Create in me a clean heart, O God, and renew a right spirit within me. Cast me not away from your presence, and take not your Holy Spirit from me. Restore to me the joy of your salvation, and uphold me with a willing spirit" (Ps. 51:10–12).

Forgiveness

Who is a God like you, who pardons sin and forgives the transgression of the remnant of his inheritance? You do not stay angry forever but delight to show mercy.

—Micah 7:18, NIV

Forgiveness is a huge part of the freedom Jesus provides for us through his sacrifice. It is spoken of often and frequently in the New Testament. Forgiveness frees us from blame, shame, and guilt. It frees us from our sins, iniquities, and transgressions. Christ will forgive all things if we come before him and ask (Matt. 7:7–8).

You might feel you've done things that aren't forgivable, but Scripture says many times over that God is gracious and compassionate. He is one who forgives and brings freedom for those who have done wrong—any kind of wrong: "Come now, let us reason together, says the Lord: though your sins are like scarlet, they shall be as white as snow; though they are red like crimson, they shall become like wool" (Is. 1:18).

Under the law of Moses, sacrifices of animals and crops had to be prepared at certain times of the year to redeem the people from sin. Now, with Jesus' perfect sacrifice, all sins can be atoned for if we just come to him. In Acts 13:38–39, Paul proclaimed this good news of forgiveness to Gentiles and fellow Israelites: Therefore, my friends, I want you to know that through Jesus the forgiveness of sins is proclaimed to you. Through him everyone who believes is set free from every sin, a justification you were not able to obtain under the law of Moses" (NIV).

Jesus is the full incarnation of God's love and compassion as we see him forgive over and over again throughout the Bible, even in the Old Testament: "If you return to the Lord, then your fellow Israelites and your children will be shown compassion by their captors and will return to this land, for the Lord your God is gracious and compassionate. He will not turn his face from you if you return to him" (2 Chron. 30:9, NIV).

Forgiveness was also emphasized by Peter when he spoke of Christ. When we repent and are baptized in water and fire, Jesus forgives: "Peter replied, 'Repent and be baptized, every one of you, in the name of Jesus Christ for the forgiveness of your sins. And you will receive the gift of the Holy Spirit'" (Acts 2:38, NIV).

Yet we are also asked to forgive others. If we do not forgive others, it can actually hinder our own forgiveness. Jesus asks us to forgive others so that the Father may forgive us. "And when you stand praying, if you hold anything against anyone, forgive them, so that your Father in heaven may forgive you your sins" (Mark 11:25, NIV).

It is clear that if God is willing to forgive us, then we should be able to forgive others too. Jesus tells a parable in which the master forgives the debt of his servant, but the servant goes out and demands repayment from another without the same mercy of his master. The master throws the servant in jail (Matt. 18:21–35). If we live in unforgiveness, isn't it like we are in jail? We are cut off from the person we cannot forgive, and part of our heart remains cut off in bitterness and misery. Wouldn't it be better to forgive and enter into the promised freedom of Christ?

This is an incredibly hard thing to do because, as humans, we can be terribly cruel to one another. Or we can misinterpret events and believe lies; the enemy is cunning. Too many good relationships have been cut short because of an offense, whether intentional or not. This can lead to all kinds of situations of broken relationships and hard, unforgiving hearts.

And sadly, unbelievably evil and terrible things have happened to people due to no fault of their own. The crime, the offense, the terrible event that has happened in your life, whether true or perceived, can eat away at you every moment of every day. If we add unforgiveness to this, we add more steel bars, seeking to keep out the person who did wrong in our eyes. In reality, the unforgiveness creates bars around us, making us prisoners.

Other times, it is the person in the mirror we need to forgive. At times like these, it is helpful to reread the Scriptures about what God thinks of you, like in chapter 7. Remember, he has massive love for you and offers forgiveness freely. So, be free from the bonds of unforgiveness by forgiving yourself and seeing the truth of who you are in Christ Jesus. Then you can enjoy life from a place of truth and freedom.

Testimony on Forgiveness

Psychologists often encourage inner child work in which the client accesses younger parts of self to give that younger part what it needed but didn't get in childhood or adolescence. By using this method, old wounds can be healed—wounds we don't consciously realize we are still carrying with us. Sometimes

I use this method to understand my feelings or reactions to circumstances in my life.

One day I was resisting something the Lord was asking me to do, and I couldn't figure out why. My rational, adult self was in love with God, devoted to his ways, and happily moving along. But as I examined my inner teen, I was surprised to find that she was angry. No, not just angry. She was furious at God and couldn't believe he would ask her to do such a thing when he hadn't been there for her when she was a teenager. She was not about to trust him to be with her in this new situation that had been put before her, and she was fuming.

I'm sure we all have stories from our teenage years that are not pleasant. I thought back to my years as a teen and knew I needed perspective, so I prayed for the Lord's help. I asked him to give me his perspective and was reminded that he never leaves us nor forsakes us (Deut. 31:6). Since Scripture is true, he was with me during my teen years, but I was just too upset and wrapped up in my own misery to see him or notice him moving in my life.

My inner teen seemed to catch on to this notion, and after some time, she remembered how much God loved her and how he was there in her time of need after all. I experienced a sort of reconciliation of the self. And though I know this sounds a little out there, working with my inner teenager helped me understand what was happening inside my heart. It allowed me to forgive Jesus, even though he was innocent. I needed to release that grudge so that his love could flow again.

We all have things we need to continue to forgive, things in our past and present that have been holding us back from love. I pray that God will lead you in his kind ways and give you grace as you work through past hurts.

Scriptures to Aid in Prayer

Meditating on Scripture or asking the Lord to guide you in understanding his Word can enrich your prayer life. These verses below can bring perspective. Below are a few Scriptures regarding forgiveness:

- "Be kind to one another, tenderhearted, forgiving one another, as God in Christ forgave you" (Eph. 4:32).
- "And whenever you stand praying, forgive, if you have anything against anyone, so that your Father also who is in heaven may forgive you your trespasses" (Mark 11:25).
- "If we confess our sins, he is faithful and just to forgive us our sins and to cleanse us from all unrighteousness" (1 John 1:9).
- "But if you do not forgive others their trespasses, neither will your Father forgive your trespasses" (Matt. 6:15).
- "Then Peter came to him and asked, 'Lord, how often should I forgive someone who sins against me? Seven times?' 'No, not seven times,' Jesus replied, 'but seventy times seven!'" (Matt. 18:21–22, NLT).
- "Judge not, and you will not be judged; condemn not, and you will not be condemned; forgive, and you will be forgiven" (Luke 6:37).

- "In him we have redemption through his blood, the forgiveness of our trespasses, according to the riches of his grace" (Eph. 1:7).
- "Pay attention to yourselves! If your brother sins, rebuke him, and if he repents, forgive him, and if he sins against you seven times in the day, and turns to you seven times, saying, 'I repent,' you must forgive him" (Luke 17:3–4).
- "I acknowledged my sin to you, and I did not cover my iniquity; I said, 'I will confess my transgressions to the Lord,' and you forgave the iniquity of my sin. Selah" (Ps. 32:5).
- "Whoever conceals his transgressions will not prosper, but he who confesses and forsakes them will obtain mercy" (Prov. 28:13).
- "And Jesus said, 'Father, forgive them, for they know not what they do.' And they cast lots to divide his garments" (Luke 23:34).
- "Bearing with one another and, if one has a complaint against another, forgiving each other; as the Lord has forgiven you, so you also must forgive" (Col. 3:13).
- "You shall not take vengeance or bear a grudge against the sons of your own people, but you shall love your neighbor as yourself: I am the Lord" (Lev. 19:18).

Chapter 13

EXPERIENCE: GROW YOUR HEART THROUGH LISTENING, DISCERNING, AND TRUSTING

Muddy water becomes clear if you only let it be still for a while.

—Dallas Willard

Experiencing God is sitting at Jesus' feet, listening, discerning, and giving him your trust. In his presence, we can realize that the God of creation is speaking to us individually in our heart. It is a joy to know he hears us and wants to talk with us.

In order to listen, we must be still and discern his voice in our heart. We can use the Bible to help us know which voice is his, for it will always speak truth. As we do these things, we learn to trust him. And trust paves the way to obedience and submission to his good will for us, for we trust he is for us and not against us (Rom. 8:31).

Listening

Psalm 46:10 says, "Be still and know that I am God." It benefits us to be still in prayer. When we settle our minds and find the place of stillness, we can hear God. But first we must distance ourselves from the clutter and noise of our daily lives. Blaise Pascal wisely said, "All of man's misfortune comes from one thing, which is not knowing how to sit quietly in a room." I see truth in this statement. When we are busy and distracted, it's easy to avoid our feelings and what God wants to show us.

A life of "busy-ness" can be a function of anxiety, for when we are busy, we can avoid our fears and questions. If we've experienced trauma, it's especially tempting to avoid our inner self. However, if unresolved trauma and repressed feelings are not addressed, they often fester, opening the door for other negative emotions and grievances to enter in.

Listen is an active word. We have to do something; namely we must quiet our mind and body. In stillness and calm, it is easier to hear God speak to our hearts. Charles Swindoll wrote of this prerequisite for finding God in our prayer time:

> We are commanded to stop (literally) . . . rest, relax, let go, and make time for Him. The scene is one of stillness and quietness, listening and waiting before Him. Such foreign experiences in these busy times! Nevertheless, knowing God deeply and intimately requires such discipline. Silence is indispensable if we hope to add depth to our spiritual life.[31]

A practical tip is to think of yourself as body, soul (mind and heart), and spirit. For the spirit to hear, the mind, heart, and body cannot be interfering. It would be like a bad connection on your mobile device. Have you ever tried to figure out how to improve your phone's signal? Sometimes it's best to be by the stairs or by a window, or maybe your connection improves in a specific room in your house. We can use the same approach to improving our connection to God in prayer. What is it that will help calm your body, mind, and spirit?

One way to quiet the body is to take a moment to actively relax by focusing on each muscle in your body from head to toe, starting with the head. Think of your forehead muscles, facial muscles, and neck muscles and completely release any tension held there; then move to your shoulders and go all the way down your body. It's amazing how much tension our bodies can hold without our awareness. This is a wonderful exercise if you have trouble sleeping too.

Next, visualize a place you enjoy and imagine yourself there. Let go of the clutter of your thoughts and the worries of your busy day. Wander to your beautiful, safe place. Listen to worship music or something peaceful and let yourself unwind so that your heart and spirit can hear more clearly.

If you have trouble with your thoughts, remember who God is; he is kind, loving, welcoming, and caring. Consider focusing on one Scripture verse. Or think of the most loving person in your life and multiply that love by as much as you can, pondering on the truth that God loves you infinitely more than this. Or simply enjoy his presence. This is the place where God can refill you, where you can bring before him the things you want to say, things you might not be tuned to when thoughts of busyness and hurry are swirling in your mind.

These moments are precious as he ministers to our hearts, comforting us and bringing us to a place of rest. Sometimes he wants to help us through an area we struggle in or show us something that has been holding us back. This is a good time to ask him questions or express the things weighing on your heart.

Openly express your concerns and listen for God, quieting yourself in patience.

Be still before the Lord and wait patiently for him; fret not yourself over the one who prospers in his way, over the man who carries out evil devices! (Ps. 37:7).

As you are in his presence, listen for his still small voice like Elijah. He stood on the mountaintop, and the Lord passed by and spoke, not in the mighty wind, a powerful earthquake, or a burning fire but in a quiet, low whisper:

> And he said, "Go out and stand on the mount before the LORD." And behold, the LORD passed by, and a great and strong wind tore the mountains and broke in pieces the rocks before the LORD, but the LORD was not in the wind. And after the wind an earthquake, but the LORD was not in the earthquake. And after the earthquake a fire, but the LORD was not in the fire. And after the fire the sound of a low whisper. And when Elijah heard it, he wrapped his face in his cloak and went out and stood at the entrance of the cave. And behold, there came a voice to him and said, "What are you doing here, Elijah?" (1 Kings 19:11–13).

Whatever might be troubling you, listen with your heart and quiet all else so that you can hear that still, small voice. God hears and responds in a variety of ways if we listen for him. It may be a small whisper like with Elijah, a sense you feel in your heart, a thought that passes in your mind that rings of truth, or even a word like Samuel heard in 1 Samuel 3:4–10.

> Then the Lord called Samuel. Samuel answered, "Here I am." And he ran to Eli and said, "Here I am; you called me." But Eli said, "I did not call; go back and lie down." So he went and lay down. Again the Lord called, "Samuel!" And Samuel got up and went to Eli and said, "Here I am; you called me." "My son," Eli said, "I did not call; go back and lie down." Now Samuel did not yet know the Lord: The word of the Lord had not yet been revealed to him. A third time the Lord called, "Samuel!" And Samuel got up and went to Eli and said, "Here I am; you called me." Then Eli realized that the Lord was calling the boy. So Eli told Samuel, "Go and lie down, and if he calls you, say, 'Speak, Lord, for your servant is listening.'" So Samuel went and lay down in his place. The Lord came and stood there, calling as at the other times, "Samuel! Samuel!" Then Samuel said, "Speak, for your servant is listening."

As you listen, use discernment to distinguish his voice. Listening is a skill, and it will become easier over time. Try not to be discouraged in the beginning. We'll talk more about discernment in the next chapter as it will help you take each thought captive as you check it against the Word of God.

Testimony on Listening

It was one of those hectic and difficult days. I came before the Lord in my prayer time, complaining in my mind, complaining in my heart. I was angry and upset about my current situation and incredulous that the person I was dealing with could be so overbearing and stubborn. How was I supposed to navigate this difficult situation? I was fuming.

My family could tell I was in a bad mood and stayed away. As I stepped into my bedroom and took a moment of quiet, I heard in my mind, *You smell putrid.* That sentence stopped me in my tracks. I thought of how Ephesians 5:1–2 says, "Therefore be imitators of God, as beloved children. And walk in love, as Christ loved us and gave himself up for us, a fragrant offering and sacrifice to God." God sees our offerings to him as a fragrant aroma, yet I was offering nothing pleasant that day. My attitude stank; it truly did, and it repelled those around me.

But fortunately God helped me gain perspective. I put on worship music and refocused on his goodness and who he is, our God and Savior. Slowly, I came back to myself and was able to rejoin my family with a renewed perspective and sweeter attitude.

I pray you find tools and methods that will help you listen to the Lord throughout your day. I pray you can find space in your day to quiet yourself and truly listen with your heart and recognize what God would say to you. Amen.

Scriptures to Aid in Prayer

Meditating on Scripture or asking the Lord to guide you in understanding his Word can enrich your prayer life. Below are a few Scriptures regarding listening:

- "Be still, and know that I am God. I will be exalted among the nations, I will be exalted in the earth!" (Ps. 46:10).
- "The Lord will fight for you, and you have only to be silent" (Ex. 14:14).
- "Be still before the Lord and wait patiently for him; fret not yourself over the one who prospers in his way, over the man who carries out evil devices!" (Ps. 37:7).
- "For God alone, O my soul, wait in silence, for my hope is from him" (Ps. 62:5).
- "Teach me, and I will be silent; make me understand how I have gone astray" (Job 6:24).
- "And the effect of righteousness will be peace, and the result of righteousness, quietness and trust forever" (Is. 32:17).
- "But let your adorning be the hidden person of the heart with the imperishable beauty of a gentle and quiet spirit, which in God's sight is very precious" (1 Pet. 3:4).
- "'The Lord is my portion,' says my soul, 'Therefore I will hope in him.' The Lord is good to those who wait for him, to the soul who seeks him. It is good that one should wait quietly for the salvation of the Lord" (Lam. 3:24–26).

- "I am humbled and quieted in your presence. Like a contented child who rests on its mother's lap, I'm your resting child and my soul is content in you" (Ps. 131:2, TPT).

Discerning

> *Attention to what goes on in the heart and to what comes forth from it is the chief work of a well-ordered Christian life. Through this attention the inward and the outward are brought into due relation with one another. But to this watchfulness, discernment must always be added, so that we may understand aright what passes within and what is required by outward circumstance. Attention is useless without discernment.*
>
> —Theophan the Recluse

At times, it's hard to know if a thought is from God, from our mind, or from the enemy. The Holy Spirit is ever speaking to us, revealing what is from the Father, but we also have our own thoughts to contend with, thoughts that can be influenced by the lies of the enemy. So how can one tell the difference between thoughts from God and thoughts of the flesh?

Scripture can be a "litmus test" for our thoughts. Through studying and memorizing Scripture, we learn the voice of God and can then discern what is true. Hebrews 4:12 speaks to this: "For the word of God is living and active, sharper than any two-edged sword, piercing to the division of soul and of spirit, of joints and of marrow, and discerning the thoughts and intentions of the heart."

For example, if a thought comes into my head that says, *You are not lovable*, I know that is a lie because Scripture tells me of God's incredible love for me: "But God shows his love for us in that while we were still sinners, Christ died for us" (Rom. 5:8). So I can recall the truth that God loves me so much he died for me and can then cast out the lie from my thoughts. I replace the lie with biblical truth.

The Bible is God's Word, so we can trust it to be accurate and true. We can take a thought captive that is not true and throw it out, just like a smelly old milk carton. Lies we tell ourselves will sour all we contact, just as rotten food will make the rest of the food in the fridge smell foul. We want to maintain freshness and keep our hearts from smelling of old lies and untruths. To walk with the Spirit, we have to be vigilant about our thought life, as Paul explained to the Corinthian church: "We destroy arguments and every lofty opinion raised against the knowledge of God, and take every thought captive to obey Christ" (2 Cor. 10:5).

As time passes and one spends more and more time in prayer, it gets easier to sense the voice of God amongst other thoughts. You see a pattern and learn to recognize the Spirit. Over time, you understand. Just as a newborn child can determine the voice of his mother, so too we can discern our Father's voice. Sometimes one might feel a "ping" or sense a shift in spirit that says, *Pay attention*. As we move with God and are more frequently in prayer with him, we can more easily discern if a thought or circumstance is legitimately important, something to ignore, or something to throw away. When you learn the voice of the Shephard, you can follow where he leads:

"To him the gatekeeper opens. The sheep hear his voice, and he calls his own sheep by name and leads them out" (John 10:3).

How can you discern if something you read or hear from someone else is true? A helpful question to ask is, does it acknowledge that Christ Jesus came from God into the flesh? Some will acknowledge that Jesus came as a prophet or wise man, but a source must recognize him as the Son of God in flesh to be a conduit of truth from the Spirit of God. First John 4:2–3 confirms that we are called to use discernment: "This is how you can recognize the Spirit of God: Every spirit that acknowledges that Jesus Christ has come in the flesh is from God, but every spirit that does not acknowledge Jesus is not from God. This is the spirit of the antichrist, which you have heard is coming and even now is already in the world" (NIV).

Discernment requires familiarity with the Word of God and the truth it holds; it requires consistent time spent listening in prayer. Over time, discernment will become easier and easier as you rightly identify truth.

Testimony on Discerning

My husband and I had been on a waiting list to adopt a child for over a year with no end in sight. We were getting discouraged about being matched with a child and were ready to give up on the process as we are older parents. Preparing for a call with our agency, we decided we would listen to what they had to say and then tell them we were done and it was time for us to walk away.

Little did we know that the agency arranged the call to ask us if we wanted to adopt twin boys. Oh, my goodness; what an amazing and surprising opportunity! My initial reaction was, *Wow, God thinks we can raise two more children. We must not have messed up too much on our first child.* I was humbled by the opportunity as I saw it as a vote of trust. But now there was a discerning process to go through because welcoming twin boys would be a huge responsibility.

My husband's initial reaction was no. He was afraid we were too old to raise two boys. I prayed and sought the Lord, and I felt I heard him say, "What do you want?" A valid question. I looked into my heart and considered God's Word to help me discern. In the Bible, children are presented as a gift from God. It is a blessing to be able to raise them. However, I didn't know how to raise twins, so I asked people I knew who had twins or were a twin themselves.

I did not want to make a decision out of fear but from an open heart. So I sat in stillness and made an effort to release thoughts of fear, like, *Can we do this?* and *Isn't two at once too much for us?* Instead, I let my heart rise to the top so I could get a sense for what my heart desired. As I sat with the Lord, I saw that my heart did desire to have more children, and I was excited and touched at the thought of having boys. So I prayed and told the Lord I would love to raise these children and was honored by the opportunity. I said, "God, if you so desire, will you move my husband's heart to desire this as well?"

Less than two weeks later, my husband and I agreed to proceed with the adoption process to joyfully add two more children to our family.

In this case, I used discernment to make a decision. It was important for me to seek the Lord in prayer, test my thinking with Scripture, and ask friends and family for insight. In the end, my husband and I had to make the decision, but God guided us. May he do the same for you as you test what you hear in prayer and seek him to discern your next right step.

Scriptures to Aid in Prayer

Meditating on Scripture or asking the Lord to guide you in understanding his Word can enrich your prayer life. Below are a few Scriptures regarding discernment:

- "Do not be conformed to this world, but be transformed by the renewal of your mind, that by testing you may discern what is the will of God, what is good and acceptable and perfect" (Rom. 12:2).
- "And it is my prayer that your love may abound more and more, with knowledge and all discernment, so that you may approve what is excellent, and so be pure and blameless for the day of Christ" (Phil. 1:9–10).
- "But solid food is for the mature, for those who have their powers of discernment trained by constant practice to distinguish good from evil" (Heb. 5:14).
- "For the word of God is living and active, sharper than any two-edged sword, piercing to the division of soul and of spirit, of joints and of marrow, and discerning the thoughts and intentions of the heart" (Heb. 4:12).
- "Give your servant therefore an understanding mind to govern your people, that I may discern between good and evil, for who is able to govern this your great people?" (1 Kings 3:9).

- "We destroy arguments and every lofty opinion raised against the knowledge of God, and take every thought captive to obey Christ" (2 Cor. 10:5).
- "Beloved, do not believe every spirit, but test the spirits to see whether they are from God, for many false prophets have gone out into the world" (1 John 4:1).

Trust

He said, "We all got secrets. I got them same as everybody else—things we feel bad about and wish hadn't ever happened. Hurtful things. Long ago things. We're all scared and lonesome, but most of the time we keep it hid. It's like every one of us has lost his way so bad we don't even know which way is home any more only we're ashamed to ask. You know what would happen if we would own up we're lost and ask? Why, what would happen is we'd find out home is each other. We'd find out home is Jesus that loves us lost or found or any which way."[32]

—Frederick Buechner

A big part of being able to pray, to truly share our hearts with God, is trust. Like in any relationship, it's a two-way street, and trust is built over time. Proverbs 3:5–6 says, "Trust in the Lord with all your heart, and do not lean on your own understanding. In all your ways acknowledge him, and he will make straight your paths."

Trusting God is easier said than done. It sometimes means we have to forgo what we think is right, what we want to do, what seems logical, or what others might agree with. When we are trusting God, we are resting on faith, not sight. The Bible is full of Scripture about why God is worthy of our trust. He is steadfast and *always* keeps his promises. He is love itself. He forgives all our wrongdoing and gave us everything to prove his love for us, though we did not deserve it.

Our lives are short (Ps. 103:15–16), but in God's infinite kindness, he lets us be a part of his mighty plan. He loves his children and knows all things. We cannot possibly imagine all the things he has for us, nor expect him to tell us everything, for how could we fathom the wonders of God? As a good parent, he tells us what we need to know, nudges us in kindness to the areas we need to work on, and brings us comfort and encouragement. We can trust his judgment as he is always working every situation for our good and is faithful to us—even when we are not.

If we "leaned on our own understanding" all the time, we might miss the wonderful things he has for us. Acknowledging that he is sovereign, faithful, and true will help us let go of fears or other hindrances that keep us from the wonderful things he wants to give us. François Fénelon writes about a believer's journey to a place of greater trust: "The closer you get to God, the more miserable things you will find in your heart. This is not a negative thing—God allows it to let you lose confidence in yourself. You will have accomplished something when you can look at your inner corruptness without anxiety or discouragement and simply trust God."[33]

When we trust that he is listening, that he is sovereign, and that his burden is light (Matt. 11:28–30), we are trusting that what he says is true. We can then move forth in his promises and let him take on the heavy burden we were trying to bear.

When we come to God in prayer, we can trust that he will hear, that he is good, and is working all things for our good (Rom. 8:28). Let God be sovereign. When he reigns and rules, he takes the burden from us. We do not need to worry then, for he is our strength. If we'll let him, he will guide and direct us, for who can know the way but God? We do not always know where he is leading or what his plans for us are. That is why he calls us to trust. He knows our hearts, and if we trust him, he will lead us, for he has good plans for us: "For I know the plans I have for you, declares the LORD, plans for welfare and not for evil, to give you a future and a hope. Then you will call upon me and come and pray to me, and I will hear you. You will seek me and find me, when you seek me with all your heart" (Jer. 29:11–13).

As we listen and discern God's voice, we learn that he is worthy of our trust. He is ever encouraging us to lean on him alone. God is such a loving God that he will protect us, even from ourselves. He can see the big picture and knows what will serve us poorly in the future or even cause danger. Someone told me once that God will sometimes push us to the side of the road, leaving us rustled, tossed, and confused, only to save us from the Mack Truck barreling down the road right at us.

God is the great Shepherd. A shepherd's key job is to care for the sheep, keep them safe, and lead them to places where they can feed and drink to grow. Sheep are naturally skittish and unwise, but the shepherd cares for each one, knowing them by name. In Psalm 23, we read that God is our shepherd and cares for our hearts, guiding us to green pastures and still waters. If we're willing to walk with him and leave behind what has been holding us back, he will keep us from fear and comfort us:

> The Lord is my shepherd; I shall not want. He makes me lie down in green pastures. He leads me beside still waters. He restores my soul. He leads me in paths of righteousness for his name's sake. Even though I walk through the valley of the shadow of death, I will fear no evil, for you are with me; your rod and your staff, they comfort me. You prepare a table before me in the presence of my enemies; you anoint my head with oil; my cup overflows. Surely goodness and mercy shall follow me all the days of my life, and I shall dwell in the house of the Lord forever.

Trusting God is a journey and something we can continually pray about and ask him to work on in our hearts. You'll find some days are better than others, but each day, we can move closer and closer to a trusting relationship with God, for he alone is the one we can truly trust.

Testimony on Trust

Sometimes I've had to trust in God and know that I hear him well. After years of practice, both getting it wrong and getting it right, I've gotten better and better at hearing his voice. As Jesus explained to the Pharisees, "My sheep listen to my voice; I know them, and they follow me" (John 10:27, NIV).

Some time ago, I was thinking about leaving a part-time job. I felt I had done all I could do, as had the organization, and we were at a stalemate. I loved the work, and the people were amazing. The programs we offered were amazing too. It was special. But as I prayed driving to a board meeting, I felt four weeks' notice come to mind. I discerned this to be his voice and felt it was right to offer my notice. I had to trust that God would take care of me during this time.

I shared my resignation with the board members, and it turned out that someone else on the team was going to leave as well. So the organization decided right then and there to dissolve. This was six weeks before COVID-19 hit the United States in a big way. God's timing was perfect. God ended this organization, an after-school program, right in the nick of time. We would not have been able to continue, and the children would have been plunged into chaos. Funding would likely have dried up, and it would have ended in a more challenging way. The dissolution of the organization put me and others in the best position to deal with the pandemic. I could not have been more grateful that I could trust God to take care of me in all these things. I pray you will learn to trust God in everything you do for he alone is trustworthy. Amen.

Scriptures to Aid in Prayer

Meditating on Scripture or asking the Lord to guide you in understanding his Word can enrich your prayer life. Below are a few Scriptures regarding trust:

- "Trust in the Lord with all your heart, and do not lean on your own understanding. In all your ways acknowledge him, and he will make straight your paths" (Prov. 3:5–6).
- "When I am afraid, I put my trust in you. In God, whose word I praise, in God I trust; I shall not be afraid. What can flesh do to me?" (Ps. 56:3–4).
- "Therefore I tell you, whatever you ask in prayer, believe that you have received it, and it will be yours" (Mark 11:24).
- "Trust in the LORD forever, for the LORD, the LORD himself, is the Rock eternal" (Isa. 26:4, NIV).
- "Blessed is the man who trusts in the Lord, whose trust is the Lord. He is like a tree planted by water, that sends out its roots by the stream, and does not fear when heat comes, for its leaves remain green, and is not anxious in the year of drought, for it does not cease to bear fruit" (Jer. 17:7–8).
- "But I have trusted in your steadfast love; my heart shall rejoice in your salvation" (Ps. 13:5).
- "And those who know your name put their trust in you, for you, O Lord, have not forsaken those who seek you" (Ps. 9:10).
- "And we know that for those who love God all things work together for good, for those who are called according to his purpose" (Rom. 8:28).
- "The fear of man lays a snare, but whoever trusts in the Lord is safe" (Prov. 29:25).

- "And without faith it is impossible to please him, for whoever would draw near to God must believe that he exists and that he rewards those who seek him" (Heb. 11:6).
- "But overhearing what they said, Jesus said to the ruler of the synagogue, 'Do not fear, only believe.'" (Mark 5:36).
- "Commit your way to the Lord; trust in him, and he will act. He will bring forth your righteousness as the light, and your justice as the noonday" (Ps. 37:5–6).

Chapter 14

TRANSFORMATION: A NEW CREATION

We pass from thinking of God as part of our life to the realization that we are part of his life.

—Richard Foster

So many wonderful things come from an active prayer life. We see transformation from a life of sin to a life of freedom. There is so much freedom and healing in his love, and a noticeable change occurs when we move into the healing and love God has for us. We are truly a new creation (2 Cor. 5:17).

Psalm 37:4 says, "Delight yourself in the LORD, and he will give you the desires of your heart." As we have an active prayer life, we can become delighted in our God, and he will give us the desires of our heart. This, to me, means he will work in our heart to make it clean and pure. And with a pure heart, our desires will be for him. So the message is not that God will give us whatever we wish for but that he will transform our heart into one that desires him and then give us his very self.

In the book, *The Seven Desires of Every Heart*, Mark and Debra Laaser list the desires of the heart: to be heard and understood, affirmed, blessed, safe, touched, chosen, and included.[34] These desires resonate with most people. And how wonderful that our God fulfills all of these things through prayer and his Word. We all desire to be heard and understood, so it is affirming to know he hears us when we pray. We can then pray for the other six core desires:

- To be affirmed: He loves us (John 3:16).
- To be blessed: He blesses us (Eph. 1:3).
- To be safe: He carries us (Isa. 46:4).
- To be touched: He touches us (Mark 1:41–42).
- To be chosen: He chose us (1 Pet. 2:9).
- To be included: He adopts us (Rom. 8:15).

So in him, truly, we are given the desires of our heart, which leads to transformation and freedom.

Transformation

> *God's recreation of his wonderful world, which began with the resurrection of Jesus and continues mysteriously as God's people live in the risen Christ and in the power of his Spirit, mean that what we do in Christ and by the Spirit in the present is not wasted. It will last all the way into God's new world. In fact, it will be enhanced there.*[35]
>
> —N. T. Wright

Part of the transformation that comes through prayer is a change of heart. If prayer is a heart-to-heart conversation, then our hearts cannot help but be transformed by being so near to God's own heart in prayer. Thanks to Jesus' death and resurrection, we can come close to him and receive his love and mercy.

When we seek him, we set aside time to devote ourselves to him. When we praise him with thanksgiving and worship, our hearts turn toward him. When we open our hearts humbly, repenting before him and seeking forgiveness, we draw closer to God. When we listen and discern, trusting what he speaks to us, then we cannot avoid transformation, for all these things shape our hearts.

Suddenly you find things that interested you and tempted you in the past are no longer alluring. You may also find yourself being kinder or more considerate of other people. You may receive compliments or find that people like being around you more. You may also find yourself hungry for God's Word and teachings about him. These are all signs that the old is gone and the new is revealed: "Therefore, if anyone is in Christ, he is a new creation. The old has passed away; behold, the new has come" (2 Cor. 5:17).

Increased Obedience

Another fruit that comes through the transformational process of prayer is increased obedience. With more and more time spent in prayer, in getting to know the Father, we are transformed, and obedience becomes natural. To know God is to love him, and as we draw closer in our relationship with God through prayer, it is easier to obey him. It becomes easier to obey because we see that he only wants our best (Rom. 8:31-32). If we trust he is working all things for our good, it is folly not to obey:

> But you can begin at once to be a disciple of the Living One—by obeying him in the first thing you can think of in which you are not obeying him. We must learn to obey him in everything, and so must begin somewhere. Let it be at once, and in the very next thing that lies at the door of your conscience! Oh fools and slow of heart, if you think of nothing but Christ, and do not yet yourselves to do his words! You but build your houses on the sand.[36]

When someone starts obeying God, others might notice a difference; something has changed within the person. A person of prayer, who now has a strong, loving relationship with God, can freely and joyfully obey God. It is no longer a chore. Even hardship for obedience is pure joy as Paul says in Romans 8:18: "For I consider that the sufferings of this present time are not worth comparing with the glory that is to be revealed to us."

A heart freely and willingly giving all to God is surrendered and open. Charles de Foucauld demonstrates this in his prayer of abandonment:

> Father, I abandon myself into your hands; do with me what you will. Whatever you may do, I thank you; I

> am ready for all, I accept all. Let only your will be done in me, and in all your creatures—I wish no more than this, O Lord. Amen.[37]

This prayer demonstrates a heart of submission, not one dominated into yielding but one that, out of love and devotion, submits its will to the will of God. This is another powerful fruit of a strong prayer life.

A heart of obedience and submission comes from love, and we grow to love God through relationship, which can be done through prayer. When we pray, we are transformed through our heart-to-heart conversation with God and see the fruit of this transformation in our obedience and submission to him and his Word. As your loves grows in him, you may find yourself feeling freer than you ever have before, as you'll read about in the next chapter.

Testimony on Transformation

When we can, some old high school friends and I will vacation together near one of our homes. It became a tight fit as our families grew, but it was so much fun to catch up since we live in different states. On one particular occasion, an old friend kept saying, "Wait a second; the old you would never say that!" After I said something kind or positive about a situation or topic we were discussing, she would stop me with that observation. It became very clear that I used to be really negative.

Throughout the weekend, I noticed that I didn't mind helping and doing the dishes, that I wanted to ensure the hosting family didn't have to be put out for any reason. We had a disgusting crock pot situation one evening, and I rolled up my sleeves and got to work. As I did this, I realized that my "old self" would never have touched something so gross. I used to avoid cleaning messes like this and would often ask my husband to do it. Now I was happy to help out.

The entire vacation, my words were more graceful. I was able to forgive grievances from my high school days as my perspective had changed. I could be more empathetic, knowing other students could have gone through difficult times like I had, or worse. Who am I to judge someone else, especially if I do not know their story? My friend kept staring in wonder at the difference in me.

It was humbling to think of how negative and miserable I must have been before God transformed me through prayer. I was grateful God was working on me, making me more like him. I pray you find yourself in a similar experience, able to see your growth and transformation as you lean into the Lord and go deeper in your relationship with him.

Scriptures to Aid in Prayer

Meditating on Scripture or asking the Lord to guide you in understanding his Word can enrich your prayer life as you lean in. Below are a few Scriptures regarding transformation:

- "Do not be conformed to this world, but be transformed by the renewal of your mind, that by testing you may discern what is the will of God, what is good and acceptable and perfect" (Rom. 12:2).

- "And we all, with unveiled face, beholding the glory of the Lord, are being transformed into the same image from one degree of glory to another. For this comes from the Lord who is the Spirit" (2 Cor. 3:18).
- "Beloved, we are God's children now, and what we will be has not yet appeared; but we know that when he appears we shall be like him, because we shall see him as he is. And everyone who thus hopes in him purifies himself as he is pure" (1 John 3:2–3).
- "And I am sure of this, that he who began a good work in you will bring it to completion at the day of Jesus Christ" (Phil. 1:6).
- "And have put on the new self, which is being renewed in knowledge after the image of its Creator" (Col. 3:10).
- "Search me, O God, and know my heart! Try me and know my thoughts! And see if there be any grievous way in me, and lead me in the way everlasting!" (Ps. 139:23–24).
- "But Jesus looked at them and said, 'With man this is impossible, but with God all things are possible'" (Matt. 19:26).
- "To put off your old self, which belongs to your former manner of life and is corrupt through deceitful desires, and to be renewed in the spirit of your minds, and to put on the new self, created after the likeness of God in true righteousness and holiness" (Eph. 4:22–24).

Chapter 15
FREEDOM: LIVING WITH NO LIMITS

The movement from illusion to prayer is hard to make since it leads us from false certainties to true uncertainties, from an easy support system to a risky surrender, and from the many 'safe' gods to the God whose love has no limits.[38]
—Henri J. M. Nouwen, *Reaching Out*

Another fruit of prayer is freedom. Our God is without limits. In prayer, we get to surrender all the things that trouble us, all the things that keep us from living a wonderful life in God's tender care. How can surrender lead to freedom? God's Kingdom is often about paradoxes: to go higher we must go lower; to live we must die to self; for sin to end, we must be born again. It's the same in this instance; being set free from sin, we are slaves to righteousness (Rom. 6:18).

So to find freedom, we must surrender our doubts, fears, and anything that hinders us. These are the things we do in our honest relationship with God: humbling ourselves; repenting for sins, iniquities, and transgressions; and forgiving others. As we pray and are honest, the things that we carried with us—resentment with a friend, wounds from a past experience, or other painful experiences—are all let go.

We surrender all these to Christ in prayer, seeking his perspective. It doesn't mean these experiences were not valid or were somehow unimportant; it simply means we submit them to Christ and will no longer let them have a hold on us. This brings freedom.

I heard it said once that Christ died for our sins, and when we do not give them to him, it is like denying his death. He died so that he could take our sins. It is his desire to carry these for us that we would walk free from sin and live in the love and joy of being with him.

As you surrender fear, anxiety, and other things that hold you back, you might find the things that used to be bothersome are no longer so. You may find that doing things that seemed scary or challenging is now simple and attainable. As you live in freedom, you may notice an increase in positive interactions with others as you act in caring or considerate ways. When all the things that used to be barriers or excuses are gone and you realize that the King of all creation is in love with you and protecting you, a whole new world opens up.

This freedom is not for just our own joy, though. We are to serve one another in love: "For you were called to freedom, brothers. Only do not use your freedom as an opportunity for the flesh, but through love serve one another" (Gal. 5:13).

I like to envision a target. Our relationship with God is at the center; from it, love flows to all in relationship with us, those closest first. As this love flows from God into us, we can more easily pour it into those around us.

May we never say, "I am free from sin now; I can do all manner of evil and ask for forgiveness and I will be forgiven." If you have gone through a true transformation with eyes fixed on God, you then love to serve. Yet be mindful to do so as a servant of God: "Live as people who are free, not using your freedom as a cover-up for evil, but living as servants of God" (1 Pet. 2:16).

So what is to be done with this freedom? We can follow Isaiah 61:1. It says that we can proclaim the good news so that those in captivity to sin, lies, guilt, shame—you name it—might be set free with the truth of God's great love, forgiveness, and mercy: "The Spirit of the Lord God is upon me, because the Lord has anointed me to bring good news to the poor; he has sent me to bind up the brokenhearted, to proclaim liberty to the captives, and the opening of the prison to those who are bound." We can spread this great news, the gospel of Jesus Christ, to all around us. And as you grab hold of this freedom, you may burst forth with joy as you proclaim this good news.

Testimony on Freedom

It's amazing the things God can bring to mind. It is sometimes difficult being a parent. I can waffle between thinking I'm doing it well to it's going okay to I'm the worst mother in the world. I was talking to the Lord and felt I heard him say, "You are a loving mother; you are not a shrew." I had to look up the word shrew and what it meant. One of its meanings, per *Merriam-Webster*, is "an ill-tempered scolding woman." I thought that was the perfect word for what I thought I was as a mother. I often thought that I was harsh and negative or always correcting and scolding my child.

I tested what I thought I heard by using the Word of God to help me discern. I asked, what does God say about me? He says he loves me, that I am a new creation: "Therefore, if anyone is in Christ, he is a new creation. The old has passed away; behold, the new has come" (2 Cor. 5:17). I took this verse to mean the old sin of being ill-tempered and angry had passed away so that I could now live as a loving mother. How do I know this is true? Because Galatians 2:20 says we were crucified with Christ and he now lives in us. He died for our sins, so now my sins are crucified. I live now by the faith that I am loved and can also be loving.

And as I live and make mistakes, God gives me grace, for I am not always proud of my behavior. I bring my sins to him for forgiveness (Jas. 4:6). Now I can live in freedom from thinking I am a shrew or living that pattern out. Instead, I live in the truth that sets me free: I am a loving mother. This truth now lives in me, and I can move forward with this truth, which forms my actions and behavior for the better. I no longer carry the lie. May God show you truth in your life that you also may be set free (John 8:32).

Scriptures to Aid in Prayer

Meditating on Scripture or asking the Lord to help guide you in the understanding of his Word can enrich your prayer life. Below are a few Scriptures regarding freedom:

- "And you will know the truth, and the truth will set you free" (John 8:32).
- "Out of my distress I called on the Lord; the Lord answered me and set me free" (Ps. 118:5).
- "So if the Son sets you free, you will be free indeed" (John 8:36).
- "For freedom Christ has set us free; stand firm therefore, and do not submit again to a yoke of slavery" (Gal. 5:1).
- "Live as people who are free, not using your freedom as a cover-up for evil, but living as servants of God" (1 Pet. 2:16).
- "I have been crucified with Christ. It is no longer I who live, but Christ who lives in me. And the life I now live in the flesh I live by faith in the Son of God, who loved me and gave himself for me" (Gal. 2:20).
- "But the one who looks into the perfect law, the law of liberty, and perseveres, being no hearer who forgets but a doer who acts, he will be blessed in his doing" (Jas. 1:25).
- "The Spirit of the Lord God is upon me, because the Lord has anointed me to bring good news to the poor; he has sent me to bind up the brokenhearted, to proclaim liberty to the captives, and the opening of the prison to those who are bound" (Isa. 61:1).
- "There is therefore now no condemnation for those who are in Christ Jesus. For the law of the Spirit of life has set you free in Christ Jesus from the law of sin and death. For God has done what the law, weakened by

the flesh, could not do. By sending his own Son in the likeness of sinful flesh and for sin, he condemned sin in the flesh, in order that the righteous requirement of the law might be fulfilled in us, who walk not according to the flesh but according to the Spirit" (Rom. 8:1–4).

- "And, having been set free from sin, have become slaves of righteousness" (Rom. 6:18).

CLOSING COMMENTS

I pray this book provides a foundation in understanding who God is, why we would want to have a relationship with him, why the heart is important to God, and how you can have a heart-to-heart conversation with God that brings freedom and transformation to your life.

Takeaways from this book:

- Prayer is a heart-to-heart conversation with God. Begin your journey to knowing him by asking God into your life and reading the Bible.
- No need to use fluffy words or formal prayers because you can speak from the heart to God.
- Jesus is after your heart and wants to be a part of your life to love you, teach you, grow you, and shape you. But it takes time and devotion to get to know him.
- If you struggle or need to realign your heart, worship and thanksgiving are always great places to start.

- A humble heart, one that is repentant and forgiving, is important for an honest prayer time that can lead to healing and renewed perspective.
- Taking time to listen for and discern God's voice will help you hear and respond to his voice as you spend more time with him.
- Above all, God is worthy of our trust. He alone is steadfast in his love and ever faithful to fulfill his Word and promises.

We have many choices before us in this life. It may take all the above efforts—and more—to stay on the path of righteousness, but God can guide us and lead us when we are in relationship with him through prayer. As the following quote from C. S. Lewis indicates, there are but two paths:

> Every time you make a choice you are turning the central part of you, the part of you that chooses into something a little different from what it was before. And taking your life as a whole, with all your innumerable choices, all your life long you are slowly turning this central thing either into a heavenly creature or into a hellish creature: either into a creature that is in harmony with God, and with other creatures, and with itself, or else into one that is in a state of war and hatred with God, and with its fellow-creatures, and with itself. To be the one kind of creature is heaven; that is, it is joy and peace and knowledge and power. To be the other means madness, horror, idiocy, rage, impotence, and eternal

> loneliness. Each of us at each moment is progressing to the one state or the other.[39]

Prayer can help us stay on a path toward being a creature of heaven as we are transformed into Christ's likeness (2 Cor. 3:18). As a relationship grows in prayer, you will find yourself more like a heavenly creature in harmony with God. I pray that you are ever moving forward in joy, peace, and knowledge, that you have a rich experience with God, and that you stay encouraged and learn to speak with our mighty God, who loves us all. And I pray Proverbs 4:23 over you, that you would "Keep your heart with all vigilance, for from it flow the springs of life" and Romans 12:12, "Rejoice in hope, be patient in tribulation, be constant in prayer." May you be blessed in your prayer journey as you discover the heart of God. Amen.

ABOUT THE AUTHOR

D. M. Stahlheber has been a prayer leader in a variety of ministries, like National Day of Prayer and NH Prayer Canopy. Stahlheber currently prays for government, ministry, and church leaders individually and with the Billy Graham Evangelical Association. When not praying, Stahlheber runs a consulting business and volunteers her time at church through community outreach, worship, or other efforts. D. M. has media experience with interviews on radio, podcasts, and TV. She also briefly produced a public TV program. This is her second book; the first is a children's story illustrating God's love to those of all ages through the story of a tiger and unicorn. Stahlheber's desire is to see a heart of prayer grow in the lives of all God's people as they come into a meaningful relationship with Jesus Christ. In her free time, she enjoys reading, working out, or playing music. D.M. feels blessed to live with her close family in beautiful New England.

ENDNOTES

1 Henri J. M. Nouwen, *With Open Hands* (Notre Dame: Ave Maria Press, 2006).

2 Albert Day, *The Captivating Presence* (Enthea Press, 2001).

3 Editorial Staff, Crosswalk. 2021. "40 Prayer Quotes - Powerful Encouragement & Inspiration!" Crosswalk. Com. Salem Web Network. March 1, 2021. https://www.crosswalk.com/faith/spiritual-life/inspiring-quotes/31-prayer-quotes-be-inspired-and-encouraged.html.

4 John H. Westerhoff and John D. Eusden, *The Spiritual Life: Learning East and West* (New York City: Seabury Press, 1982).

5 Ibid.

6 *St. Margaret Mary Alacoque*

7 Nouwen, *With Open Hands.*

8 Frederick Buechner, *Listening to Your Life: Daily Meditations with Frederick Buechner* (San Francisco, HarperOne, 1992).

9 Miroslav Volf, *A Public Faith* (Grand Rapids: Brazos Press, 2011).

10 C. S. Lewis, *Lion, the Witch and the Wardrobe* (Grand Rapids: Zondervan, 2009).

11 Donald G. Bloesch, *The Struggle of Prayer* (Colorado Springs: Helmers & Howard Publishers, 1989).

12 J. K. Rowling, *Harry Potter and the Sorcerer's Stone* (New York City: Scholastic Press, 1998).

13 "Fatherless Statistics for the United States," *Fatherhood Factor*, June 11, 2010, https://fatherhoodfactor.com/us-fatherless-statistics/.

14 Carlo Carretto, *The God Who Comes* (Ossining: Orbis Books, 1974).

15 Ibid.

16 Abraham Joshua Heschel, 1976. *God in Search of Man : A Philosophy of Judaism* (New York City: Farrar, Straus and Giroux, 1976).

17 Henri J. M. Nouwen, *The Wounded Healer: Ministry in Contemporary Society* (New York City: Doubleday, 1979).

18 "How to Make Friends? Study Reveals Time It Takes," *The University of Kansas*, March 6, 2018, https://news.ku.edu/2018/03/06/study-reveals-number-hours-it-takes-make-friend.

19 Carretto, *The God Who Comes.*

20 *Lexico*, s.v. "devotion." Accessed July 28, 2021, https://www.lexico.com/en/definition/devotion.

21 *Lexico*, s.v. "observance." Accessed July 28, 2021, https://www.lexico.com/en/definition/observance.

22 Dr. Caroline Leaf, *Switch On Your Brain: The Key to Peak Happiness, Thinking, and Health.* (Ada: Baker Books, 2015).

23 Charles R. Swindoll, *Intimacy with the Almighty* (Nashville: Thomas Nelson, 1998).

24 Howard Thurman, *The Inward Journey* (Richmond: Friends United Press, 2007).

25 Evelyn Underhill, *The Spiritual Life* (Eastford: Martino Fine Books, 2013).

26 Glenn Clark, *I Will Lift Up Mine Eyes* (New York City: HarperCollins, 1984).

27 *Merriam-Webster*, s.v. "repent." Accessed July 14, 2021. https://www.merriam-webster.com/dictionary/repent.

28 *The Ancient Hebrew Research Center*. s.v. "sin."Accessed July 14, 2021. https://www.ancient-hebrew.org/definition/sin.htm.

29 *Merriam-Webster*, s.v. "iniquity." Accessed July 14, 2021. https://www.merriam-webster.com/dictionary/iniquity.

30 *Merriam-Webster*, s.v. "transgression." Accessed July 14, 2021. https://www.merriam-webster.com/dictionary/transgression.

31 Swindoll, *Intimacy with the Almighty*.

32 Frederick Buechner, *The Book of Bebb* (San Francisco: HarperOne, 2001).

33 François Fénelon, *The Seeking Heart* (Jacksonville: SeedSowers, 1992).

34 Mark Laaser, *The Seven Desires of Every Heart* (New York City: HarperCollins Christian, 2008).

35 N. T. Wright, *Surprised by Hope: Rethinking Heaven, the Resurrection, and the Mission of the Church* (San Francisco: HarperOne, 2008).

36 Rolland Heinand George MacDonald, *Creation in Christ: Unspoken Sermons* (Vancouver: Regent College Publishing, 2004).

37 "Blessed Charles de Foucauld: Praying His Prayer of Self-Abandonment," *Papal Artifacts,* July 12, 2020, https://

www.papalartifacts.com/december-1-on-the-feast-of-blessed-charles-de-foucauld-his-prayer-of-abandonment/.

38 Henri J. M. Nouwen, 1986. *Reaching Out: The Three Movements of the Spiritual Life* (New York City: Doubleday, 1986).

39 C. S. Lewis, *Mere Christianity* (Grand Rapids: Zondervan, 2001).